ARCHERY

SKILLS

TACTICS

TECHNIQUES

CROWOOD SPORTS GUIDES

ARCHERY

SKILLS

TACTICS

TECHNIQUES

Deborah Charles

THE CROWOOD PRESS

First published in 2015 by
The Crowood Press Ltd
Ramsbury, Marlborough
Wiltshire SN8 2HR

www.crowood.com

British Library Cataloguing-in-Publication Data
A catalogue record for this book is available from the British Library.

ISBN 978 1 84797 959 9

Acknowledgements
Thanks to Aquarius Archery Club and my fellow archers.

All photographs are by the author.

Typeset by Jean Cussons Typesetting, Diss, Norfolk

Printed and bound in India by Replika Press Pvt Ltd

CONTENTS

INTRODUCTION

Archery is a sport that can be enjoyed by everyone – men and women of any age, and whether they are able bodied or disabled. It may look like strength is needed to pull a bow, but the success of archery relies more on technique than pure muscle power.

The aim of this book is to explain to the beginner the art of archery and to guide the improver in ways that will help advance their progression. The basic form of every archer is essentially the same across all disciplines of the sport so this book will give you the foundations you need to shoot a bow safely and competently. The topics covered concentrate on recurve target archery, which is the most commonly practised style in clubs around Great Britain and is the basis for the Olympic competition.

As the archer becomes more accomplished they will learn there are many differences in opinion on technique. Where possible I have covered the variations, because ultimately, archery is a sport of the individual. What works for you may not work for someone else. This is where the fun and the challenge lie.

Through the ages

Prehistoric roots

The bow and arrow have been used since prehistoric times. Historically, archery was used for hunting, enabling the spear thrower to become a much more proficient hunter. Evidence shows bows were adapted for combat across many continents right up until the invention of firearms.

Hunters

The earliest proof of bow and arrows being used by hunters comes from stone-age cave paintings that date back to 20,000BC and the discovery of arrowheads from before 25,000BC. Around this time, archers were adding feathers to their arrows to aid flight and accuracy. The oldest bow found was in

The constellation of Sagittarius.

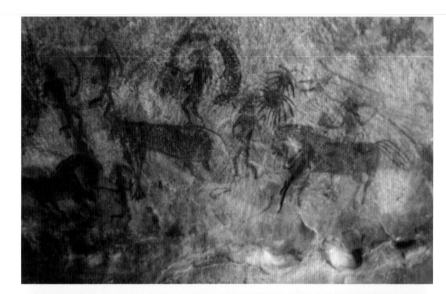

Cave painting showing hunters using bows and arrows.

Northern Europe and dates from around 9,000BC. Although a simple wooden bow, the craftsmanship shows a high level of sophistication that adheres to design principles still used today.

Military use

With the development of the composite bow, constructed from wood, animal horn and sinew, the recurve bow became a formidable military weapon. Being shorter, but much more powerful, enabled the bow to be shot from horseback or from a chariot, sending arrows 200m or more. Bows were used to defeat enemies across Persia, Egypt, India, China and Japan. Attila the Hun and his Mongols dominated much of Europe and Asia, whilst Turkish armies using bow and arrows overwhelmed the Crusaders. The Parthinians, who were great horseback archers, combined speed, agility and ingenuity to defeat their enemies. Under the pretence of retreating they would swivel around in their saddle and shoot backwards at full gallop, defeating their unsuspecting foes. This trick gave rise to the term 'a parting shot'.

During the medieval period, the English Longbow decided many a battle, particularly in the Hundred Years War. These bows were made from a single piece of yew, stood nearly two metres tall and had draw weights of over 100lb. In combat archers would shoot as many as five arrows per minute. With as many as 5,000 archers on the English side in Agincourt, 50,000 arrows

Horse archers shooting backwards.

The Battle of Agincourt.

unleashed in two minutes of a battle would have a huge impact on the outcome.

Archery took skill and practice. Kings officially banned football, bowls and golf so that archery would be practised instead. However, the invention of the musket and the advances of gunfire rendered the bow obsolete on the battle frontline by the seventeenth century.

Mythological archers

Archery has played an integral part in many myths. Odysseus won the hand of Penelope by shooting an arrow through the holes in ten axe hooks; Eros more commonly known as Cupid, shot arrows of desire; whereas Apollo shot arrows carrying the plague, and Paris shot an arrow that wounded Achilles in his heel.

The bow and arrow also feature more recently in folklore, from the heroic outlaw Robin Hood to the defiant William Tell, who with a single shot split an apple that rested on his son's head. The archer also appears in our night skies in the constellation of Sagittarius.

Archery as sport

Despite the demise of archery for military purposes, it remained popular for hunting and as a recreational activity, especially among the aristocracy, and many archery societies were set up during the seventeenth and eighteenth centuries. However, it was not until the formation of the Grand National Archery Society (mid-nineteenth century) and the establishment of set rules and rounds that the pastime of archery was turned into the modern sport of today.

Interest in archery waned with the arrival of croquet and tennis, but in the twentieth century advances in technology brought archery back as a popular pursuit. New materials enabled the archer to become more accurate and consistent, but the real revolution in the sport came from the development of the compound bow; this design, featuring levers and pulleys, enables a very high draw weight to be pulled with minimal effort. This style of bow is rapidly growing in popularity but is also helping to revive an interest in the traditional styles at the same time.

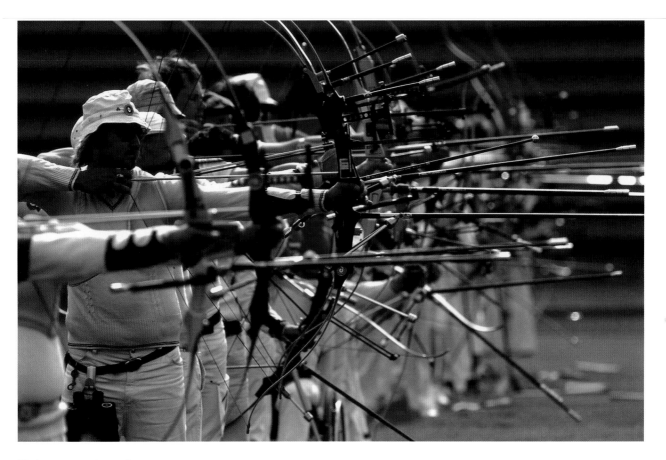

Modern recurves being shot.

Other types of archery

The longbow and barebow usually rely on instinctive shooting, which involves releasing the arrow without consciously calculating the distance.

Longbow

The most famous bow is probably the English longbow. This is a wooden bow shot with wooden arrows which use feathers as fletches. It is basically shooting one piece of stick from another. The accuracy relies purely on the archer's skill. To hit a target the archer often has to aim way off to the side or right up in the sky. There are some very skilled longbow archers who have an amazing accuracy with this basic bow. Longbows can be fun because it becomes less about scores and more just about hitting the boss, which gives a great sense of achievement.

Barebow

A barebow is a recurve bow that is free from sight or sight marks. There are two styles of aiming: string walking, which involves moving your finger position on the string to achieve accuracy; or gap shooting, which is much more instinctive and takes time to master. It is very impressive to watch an instinctive archer.

Compound bow

Compound bows are designed for maximum accuracy. They use a cam lever system and a mechanical trigger and shoot heavy poundage. Almost anything to assist the archer is allowed on these bows provided it is not electrical. These bows are very popular for hunting in the US, and they are becoming more popular in the UK, both in field and target archery.

Field archery

All of the above types of bow are particularly popular among field archers. This discipline involves a number of targets placed at different distances in

LEFT: The longbow.

RIGHT: The bare bow.

woodland or rough ground. The archers set off in groups and walk around a marked course, shooting at targets as they go. There are marked distance shoots and unmarked shoots. The most popular rounds are shot with animal pictures as targets or with actual 3D animals placed in the terrain. Very often an archer will shoot up and down dale, across ravines, over water and through foliage. It is challenging and therefore very rewarding.

The compound bow.

Field shooting is popular in Europe and is gaining ground in the UK.

The modern era

Nowadays, archery is still used for hunting, as a martial art, an enjoyable pastime and as an ever-prevalent competitive sport. During the 2012 Olympics, archery was one of the most popular sports watched on television, mainly due to changes in the competition format that had been put in place to make the matches more exciting to spectators.

South Korean success

Since the South Koreans first entered the Olympics, they have dominated the archery medal tables, especially within the women's competition. The Korean women have won almost every medal since 1984. Park Sung Hyun is considered among the world's best. She is a world record holder, who won three golds and one silver Olympic medal before retiring. The form and

technique of the South Korean archers have been credited to their coach Kisik Lee, who focused on the biomechanics of shooting. His success has led to his coaching style being adopted by many of the world's national teams at the highest levels.

Field shoot.

PART I
AN INTRODUCTION TO ARCHERY

CHAPTER 1

GETTING STARTED

Finding a club

Archery in the UK is a club sport, so the best way to start shooting is to find the nearest club. Visit the Archery GB website run by the governing body of archery in the UK. They have a club finder where you can input your postcode and find the contact details of local clubs. With over 1,200 clubs across the UK there is probably a club near you. A web search will also reveal nearby clubs or the nearest archery shop that will be able to help.

When starting archery you will be asked to join an induction course. The beginner's course will introduce you to the basics of the sport, the disciplines of safe shooting and the enjoyment of a sport that has a huge history. Most archery clubs run regular beginner courses taught by experienced archers who have completed a coaching course. There are often come-and-try days or taster sessions too. Many archery shops also have shooting ranges and run courses throughout the year. The cost of the course will vary from club to club, but they will provide you with equipment, tuition and insurance. If, after your beginner course, you decide you would like to continue with the sport you will have to join the club and become a member of Archery GB. This is a requirement for all archers in the UK, as it provides insurance cover for you and the club.

Archery clubs vary in terms of where and when they shoot, so this can be a factor when considering what club to join. Many clubs shoot outdoors and indoors, whereas some clubs are limited to shooting indoors at a sports or school hall. Some fortunate clubs have twenty-four-hour access to an outdoor shooting range such as a field or sports ground, but other clubs are restricted to set times or days of the week. Typically, most outdoor clubs shoot at an indoor venue during the winter. It is also sometimes worth asking who shoots regularly. Sometimes a club can have a lot of members, but only a few who shoot frequently. Some clubs also charge a small fee for every time you shoot. Whatever club you choose to join, all clubs are friendly and welcoming to newcomers.

Governing bodies

Archery GB is the National Governing Body for all forms of archery in the UK and Northern Ireland. It organizes tournaments, supports training and coaching programmes as well as running a website that provides information on clubs, competitions, rules and the latest news in the sport. Archery GB is actually the trading name of the Grand National Archery Society (GNAS), which was founded back in 1861 in order to promote archery throughout the kingdom (and many archers still refer to them as GNAS).

Beginners' day.

Royal British bowmen, 1822.

Archery GB is affiliated to World Archery (WA), the world governing body for the sport of archery, based in Lausanne, Switzerland. WA regulates and promotes the sport across 150 member associations throughout the world. It runs many international competitions and is affiliated to the Olympic International Committee. WA used to be FITA (Fédération Internationale de Tir à l'Arc) that was originally founded in 1931 with the sole aim of running regular competitions and returning archery to the Olympic Games. In 1972 archery was successfully reinstated in the Olympic Programme and has been an Olympic sport ever since. In 2011, to celebrate the organization's 80th anniversary and its modern vision, the name FITA was changed to World Archery. In 2014 FITA competitions were re-named WA competitions.

What to expect on a beginner's course

On a beginner's course you will be fitted out with a bow and arrows and receive instruction on the basics of how to hold a bow and shoot an arrow. Most clubs supply basic equipment that you can borrow for the course duration and often a little longer. After the first few months or so you would then be expected to purchase your own equipment. It is advisable not to buy equipment too early on because your form will not be developed, but to wait until your style has settled and then your choice of bow should last you your first year, if not longer.

There is no specific clothing required for archery apart from comfortable shoes or trainers (No open toed shoes are allowed on an archery range). A snug fitting top is also advisable since loose or baggy clothing can cause interference with the bow or the path of the arrow.

Bows

Bows are either right-handed or left-handed. A right-handed bow is held in your left hand and drawn back using your right arm whereas a left-handed bow is held in your right hand and drawn back using your left arm. Most right-handed people feel comfortable with a right-handed bow.

There is another important factor that comes into play when selecting your bow, however, and that is eye dominance. Aiming is crucial in archery; therefore it is essential to establish which eye you will use to line up the arrow and the target. Your dominant eye will naturally become your aiming eye and will determine whether you will shoot a right or left-handed bow.

The way to establish eye dominance is through a simple test. Extend your arms out in front of you and form a small triangular hole with your hands. Look through this hole and fix focus on a small, static object in the distance such as a faraway target. Close one eye. If you close

Eye dominance.

Eye dominance.

your left eye and you can still see the target framed by your triangle then you are right-eyed dominant. If you close your right eye and can still see the target then you are left eye dominant. A right-eyed person should shoot a right-handed bow and left-eye dominant should use a left-handed bow. Another way to test this out is to move your hands up to your eye whilst still keeping the target in vision. You will find that you will bring your hands toward your dominant eye.

Arrows

You will be given a set of arrows, normally six. Arrows must be the right length to suit the archer, not too long and not too short. This is called your draw length. The best way to choose the correct arrow length is to hold an arrow straight in front of you with the back end of the arrow in the centre of your chest and both arms outstretched forming a V shape with the palms together and fingers pointing forward. The point of the arrow should stretch a few inches beyond the tips of your fingers. Never shoot with an arrow that is too short for you as this can be dangerous.

Beginner's arrows are normally aluminium or wood. Each arrow has a metal point at one end called a pile or point and a grooved joint called a nock at the other. In order to shoot the arrow the nock needs to be to clipped or 'nocked' on to the string at the 'nocking point' which is a marked point on the string that makes sure the arrow releases straight and from the same point every time. Arrows have three fletches or vanes on them. These help steer the arrow and are made from either plastic or traditional feathers. One fletch is usually a different colour to the other two and is known as the cock feather or cock vane. It is lined

Arrow length.

up on the arrow in such a way that it points away from the bow every time you attach the arrow to the string; this makes sure the fletches do not hit the bow on release and regulates the variables for every arrow shot.

Protective gear

You will also be given:

- A bracer which fits on your forearm to protect your arm and keep clothing out of the way of the bow string.
- A bow or finger sling that fits around the bow at the handgrip, so that the bow does not fall to the ground while you are shooting.
- A finger tab that protects your fingers from the string when you release the arrow.

Quiver and boss

The quiver holds your arrows. This can either be a ground quiver or one

Close-up of a Jazz arrow.

Bracer, finger sling, finger tab and arrows.

that is attached to a belt around your waist or back.

The boss is the arrow stop that you shoot at, which is made of dense straw or foam. The target face is the piece of paper stretched over the boss that consists of different coloured scoring rings. The middle is highest scoring and is usually yellow/gold in colour (sometimes referred to as the custard).

Procedure at the archery range

All archery ranges have to adhere to safety specifications, so they are always laid out on the same pattern with over-shoot distances in place behind and to the side of the targets. Targets are set at one end, with the shooting and waiting line at the other.

Archers step up to the shooting line to fire their bow. When they have shot they step back to behind the waiting line. This makes it very clear to everyone when all archers have finished shooting, and allows archers to collect their arrows safely. Often there is a field captain who oversees the line. Shooting commences with a single blow of the whistle, whereas two blows of the whistle signals that all shooting has

finished and arrows can be collected. In more casual shooting situations there is no captain per se so it is up to the individual archers to make sure it is safe. All archers follow the same safety procedures and communicate with each other using the word 'Commence' or 'Okay' for shooting to begin and 'Collect' once everyone has finished. All equipment is kept behind the waiting line to prevent mishaps.

Basic safety rules

Before shooting
- The arrow should only be put into the bow when on the shooting line.
- The bow should be pointing toward the target or the ground when an arrow is nocked. A bow should never be pointed at anything other than the target when being drawn.
- The bow should never be drawn pointing up into the air. Mistakes can happen, and an arrow that is accidentally released pointing sky high can easily travel over the safety distances.

During shooting
- An archer must not step over the shooting line to retrieve even a dropped arrow when other archers are shooting.
- 'Fast' is shouted to stop all shooting if someone has spotted a potentially dangerous situation, such as a walker crossing the field or a stray dog behind the target. When 'Fast' is called then everyone should remove their arrows from the bow.

Range layout.

After shooting
- When you walk to the target, do not run. Carry arrows in a quiver or point them end downwards.
- When pulling arrows from the boss check that no one is standing directly behind you. Likewise do not stand directly behind someone else who is pulling arrows. It takes a little force to remove an arrow from the boss and the nock end of an arrow is rather sharp, easily resulting in an arm or eye being poked. This is a painful mistake that is quite common due to eager archers pulling their arrows whilst others are still looking for their arrows in the target. (It can be quite confusing when a number of archers are shooting lots of arrows at the same target.) It is good shooting etiquette for archers to ask their fellow shooters if it is 'Okay to pull', to make sure everyone has scored and is happy to stand back.

Arrows in the boss..

CHAPTER 2

BUYING YOUR OWN EQUIPMENT

The bow

Most clubs have limited beginner's bows, so once you have been shooting a while you will need to buy your own equipment. These days, beginner bows are incredibly good, reasonably priced and perfectly apt for your first year of archery.

Archery is a sport with a lot of variables, so the best way to begin is to find a bow that suits you, and generally what suits you is what feels comfortable. Feeling relaxed, confident and happy with your equipment is a great start. 'Trust in your bow' is one of the best bits of advice I was given. Generally, your bow will serve you well – it's you that will need the work! Therefore, if you buy something you like shooting and that feels right then you are well on your way to developing good form.

By the time you are ready to purchase your first bow and arrows you will probably already have been shooting with a club bow and arrows that suit your size and strength, so you will have some idea of what type of bow and arrows you are looking for. Even so, it can still be a little daunting. The assistance of an archery shop, or an experienced archer, is advisable for helping you select your first bow and arrows. Good secondhand bows can be found on eBay or similar websites, and many club archers have old equipment to sell, but it is best to get some guidance before making a financial commitment. Visiting a shop is a good idea just because you can try out a few different bows before making your purchase and they will help set it up correctly too.

The best bow is one that you can pull comfortably, so you can shoot with ease and accuracy, but which will also enable you to progress as a shooter. Take your time in choosing your equipment. Every bow shoots a little differently to the next. How much money you are willing to spend is also a factor, but be warned, the most expensive bow and arrows will not make you a better archer; in fact they will probably hinder you. Often the top-end bows are less forgiving, and as a beginner you will not have the skill to control them.

Remember too, that there are a number of additional items you will need to buy, such as an arrow rest, finger tab, quiver, stand and bag – bow and all its components is not the easiest equipment to transport around.

Riser and limbs

Most recurve bows are take-down bows that consist of a riser and limbs. Bows are measured by their length and weight, with standard bows usually made up of a 23", 25" or 27" riser. Limbs come in three lengths: short (54–66"), medium (68") and long (70"). Any combination of limb can be put on any size riser to accommodate the shooter's physique and strength, but they must be of the same system. The International Limb Fitting (ILF) used to be standard, but more recently Formula bows, which have a Paralever system, have entered the market. An ILF limb only fits an ILF riser, and Formula limbs only fit a Formula bow. Every limb is marked with the weight and length.

Risers on the waiting line.

Riser

Risers come in a variety of materials, weights and styles and generally will stay with you for a lot longer than your first limbs. They also come in a lot of different colours and finishes, although the UK stockists do not always stock everything you will see on a website. Archers often choose a riser purely because they like the look of it and it feels good. You will be surprised how important this is to your shooting. Archery is very much a mental game. If you like your riser you will want to shoot it.

The grip of a riser can make a big difference to how the bow sits, and feels, in your hand. Someone with large hands might prefer a wider grip than someone with a petite hand. It is crucial to have a comfortable grip that suits your hand.

There are high, medium and low grips, angular or rounded grips and plastic or wooden grips. These days, grips are often interchangeable: it is easy to swap a grip by loosening the two screws either side and popping it off the riser, so once you have been shooting for a while you can experiment a little.

Limbs

The majority of limbs are constructed from laminated wood or the more modern materials of synthetic foam and carbon, which make for lighter, faster and more consistent limbs. Favourable

> **PERSONAL TIP**
>
> I have a tendency to hold the bow too tightly, so I prefer a rounded grip with a thin neck, which helps lessen the effect of this habit.

manufacturers are Hoyt, Win & Win, SF Archery, Samick and Kaya. The smaller European companies Border and Ukkha are also popular.

Bow weight

To work out what bow and limbs you require depends on your draw weight – the force needed to 'draw' the bow. This is also called your poundage. You should be able to comfortably shoot the bow for a couple of hours. If the bow is too heavy you will start to lose accuracy because you do not have the strength to maintain control of the bow, whereas a bow that is too light may limit you to short distances only, which will soon become frustrating.

The draw weight measurement of a limb is standardized to a 28-inch arrow length and is marked on the bottom of every limb. The rule of thumb is that for every draw inch over 28" the weight of the limb will increase by 2 pounds and

Limb markings.

every inch under will decrease by 2 pounds; so a tall person with long arms using a 30" arrow will pull much more poundage than a small archer with short arms using a 26" arrow despite having identical weight limbs. For this reason, archers will often ask: 'What's your poundage?' or 'What's on your fingers?' rather than ask what weight your limbs are. You can increase the weight of each limb by winding the bolts of the bow in or decrease the weight by winding the bolts out, which means you can buy a limb that you can 'wind up' in poundage as your form and strength improves. However, the adjustable poundage is only 10 per cent of the marked weight on the limb, so a 26lb bow can only increase to 28lb whereas a 36lb bow can increase to 40lb.

Sight

A good sight should be easy to use and should be incremental in adjustment. It has to move up and down to allow for distance and from side to side to allow for adjustments for wind. A cheap sight can be good as a starter, but can become irksome after only a few months. The bow undergoes quite a lot of vibration

Grips.

LEFT: Sight.

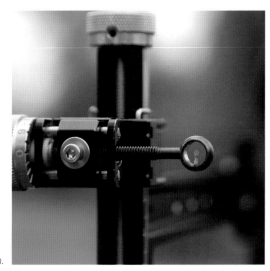

RIGHT: Sight pin.

when it is shot, so thumbscrews often come loose or sometimes lose the ability to tighten up properly. You pay for good engineering, so top end sights are expensive but well worth it. However, this means they are not often found on the secondhand market.

Sight pin

There are many different sight pins with variable inserts, from pins with circles to fluorescent squares and light-gathering filaments. Most archers begin with the standard pin and then try out the variations until they settle on what they like. Often different sight pins are supplied with the sight so you can play around.

Stabilizer system

As you start to shoot longer distances a long rod and side rods can aid the balance of the bow and help reduce vibration. The long rod reduces rotation on the vertical and horizontal planes, whereas the side bars help stop left and right tilting. Adding a rod to the top of the riser can help reduce vibration felt in the hand and the sight. You can even get tiny sight weights to stop vibration of the sight bar. Do bear in mind that most archers you see in international competition are probably shooting a lot

more poundage than you, and more poundage means an increase in vibration, so do not feel the need to overload your bow with weights just yet. It is good to begin shooting without these additions, which really come into their own once you move to longer distances.

String

Each string is made with two loops; a larger loop at the top and a smaller loop at the bottom and should have about 12–20 twists in it so it gives a nice, rounded consistency for shooting. The reinforced section on the ends and the

middle is called the serving, which helps protect the string where it hits the bow. This is just an extra layer of string. Strings come in different materials, different strands and colours, as do serving materials.

Strings also come in different lengths relative to your bow size, so do check your bow's recommendation in the manual or on the manufacturer's website.

Many clubs have string jigs, string material and keen archers who will show you how to make your own string. In the meantime, you can buy ready-made strings from websites or from archery shops, which often have deals with very practised archers who will make you

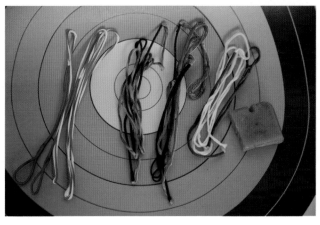

Strings.

personalized strings in your colours of choice.

The more strands a string has the slower but more stable it shoots, whereas with fewer strands archer errors become more noticeable. As a general guide, 16–18 strands are for bows up to 35lb, 18–20 strands for 35–40lb, 20+ strands for 40–45lb. Dacron is a popular starter string, although this is a rather slow, stretchy string, so I would recommend starting out with another readily available material such as BCY-8125 or Fast Flight.

Bow stringing. Hook the larger loop of the string over the top limb, secure the pocket of the stringer over the bottom limb and place the open end of the stringer over the top limb and string.

HANDY HINT

The term 'another string to my bow' originates from the mid fifteenth century when archers in battle would carry a reserve string in case their first snapped.

How to string a bow

Use a bow stringer. Some archers brace the limbs into the arch of the foot and press against the top limb to release the pressure, but nowadays with Formula fittings this can easily result in a limb flipping off or rebounding into your face, so best not do it. Stringing a bow seems awkward to start, but it becomes much easier the more you do it.

Strings come with a slightly larger loop at the top end. Begin by hooking this larger loop over the top limb. Now, secure the smaller loop into the groove at the tip end of the lower limb. Sometimes pinching the string in a little helps secure it in place. Put the pocket end of the stringer over the lower limb and the open end over the top limb and over the string hook.

Put your foot right on to the middle of the bow stringer (not just the toe, as sometimes it can spring free with the effort) and pull the riser up toward you so that the limbs bend. Move the larger loop of the string toward the tip of the top limb, until it slots into the groove. If the string is not in place at either end it will ping off, so it is advisable to double check the tension of the string with your fingers whilst looking back at the other end to check the limb tips are moving.

Now gently release the riser back

ABOVE: Move the larger loop into the groove on the top limb

BOTTOM LEFT: Checking tension.

BOTTOM RIGHT: Bow strung.

down to your foot and you will find you have strung your bow. Twang the string back a few inches so the limbs settle into place.

To unstring a bow do the same thing in reverse. Be careful when the limbs are wet because the bow stringer will slip down the limb and jolt the string out of place. Drying the limbs will stop this.

Brace height

Check the bow's guideline for the correct brace height recommendations. Brace height is measured from the button to the bowstring, or the deepest part of the handle to the string, using a bow gauge. Whichever way you choose to measure your bow, always measure it from the same point to keep consistency.

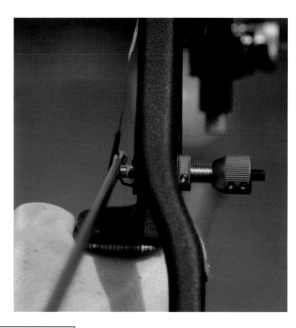

Button, arrow rest, clicker.

PERSONAL TIP

It is best to put on your string at the recommended brace height but then after shooting a little, say thirty arrows or so, check it again, because once the string settles into the bow it often drops a little in brace height. I usually string my bow about 2mm above the brace height, knowing that it will settle down to my desired brace height.

Brace height gauge.

Bow accessories

Button

A button is there to help hold the arrow in the right place. You do not have to purchase a button when you begin, but it is advisable. You can change the setting and stiffness of the button by using the small allen keys supplied with it. To move the actual button position in the bow, undo the grub screw on the middle band with the supplied allen keys so you can move it up or down.

Arrow rest

There are many different arrow rests: plastic, metal, stick-on, magnetic. For your first bow the simple white Hoyt super rest is really good and incredibly robust. They have a little curve on them to help keep the arrow in place, which can be very helpful for a beginner, especially in windy conditions when the arrow can be blown off the rest. Occasionally some shops snip off the very curved, thin bit so it does not catch the arrow on release.

Clicker

It is best to develop your form and find your draw length before introducing a clicker. Most archers want to improve as quickly as they can and often adopt a clicker far too early, but if not set up correctly the clicker can start to dominate the shot cycle. A beginner can easily lose all sense of their form because they are just concentrating on when the click is going to happen.

Arrows

Arrow shafts come in wood, fibreglass, aluminium and carbon. They are measured in terms of length, weight and spine. Arrows are matched to your bow weight rather than the other way around. Your club will usually supply your first arrows, but after time you will probably need to purchase your own set.

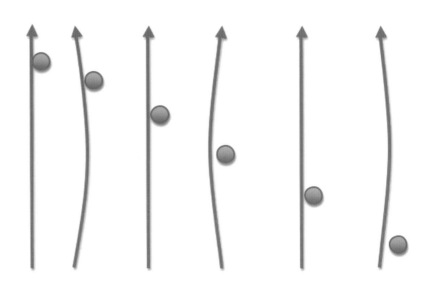

Arrow bend.

Choosing the arrow that suits you

Arrows are hugely variable. Two archers of similar height and build, shooting the same poundage and an identical bow, will not necessarily end up shooting the same arrows. Which arrow spine suits you is entirely related to your bow and your technique. There are many conversations on the line over arrows.

Arrow flight and the Archer's Paradox
Arrows do not fly straight; they bend as they travel forward. This is called the Archer's Paradox, a term originated in the 1930s by a Dr R.P. Elmer, who was intrigued as to why an arrow placed on the side of the bow could hit a target straight ahead.

The explanation is this: On release, the bow string slides away from the fingers, which creates a forward motion that sends the arrow forward, but at the same time creates a sideways movement which forces the arrow to bend in one direction. (The smoother the archer's release, the lesser the sideways deflection and lesser the bend.) The arrow basically bends around the riser. The arrow is also propelled forward with a force from the release that makes the back of the arrow try to move faster than the front of the arrow.

The arrow reacts to both forces by flexing one way and then the other, until it hits the target. The paradox is that although the arrow is pointing away from the target it will fly in a straight line to the point of aim. There is some great slow motion footage online that has captured this conundrum.

Spine
Spine is basically the stiffness of the arrow shaft. There are actually two different spines of an arrow: the static and the dynamic. The static spine is the amount of flex in the arrow shaft, whereas the dynamic spine is the way an arrow reacts to the stored energy of the bow as it is fired. The dynamic spine is influenced by many factors – such as the arrow weight and length, the way the arrows are released by the archer's fingers, the type of string being shot – so it is hugely variable. Therefore, the static spine is the constant that everyone refers to.

Weight
Every aluminium arrow has a four number numeric marked on the shaft, which refers to the arrow's diameter and the thickness.

The outside diameter is measured in 64ths of an inch and the wall thickness of the arrow shaft in thousanths of an inch, so an 1816 shaft means the outside diameter is 18/64ths of an inch and the wall thickness is 16/1000th of an inch. Carbon arrows are based on actual spine deflections, which is relative to the amount of sag an arrow has when a

Arrow shaft numbers.

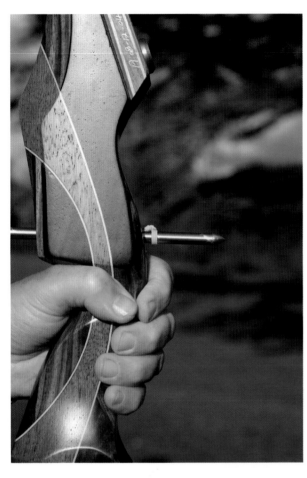

Elastic band on uncut arrow.

wide range of sizes, are very regular on release, fantastically durable and cheap. They can even be straightened out after accidental hits in the wood – which is inevitable for beginners.

Once you have been shooting for a while you will most probably want to move onto an arrow that will help you become more accurate at the further distances. The most popular choice is a carbon and aluminium mix. These are lighter and thinner which means there is less wind resistance; therefore they maintain velocity at longer distances. 'Allys' are heavier and remain in the air longer which makes them more open to the effects of wind at longer distances. However, depending on your poundage a good set of aluminium arrows should get you to 70 metres – even if you have to turn your sight inside out.

The Easton Chart

There are many makes of arrows, but for recurve target archery most people across the UK shoot Easton arrows, which are readily available and come in a wide range of spines. The Easton Chart is the Holy Grail that everyone refers to when selecting arrows.

If you sit between groupings then err on the stiff side. A stiffer arrow will be more forgiving and accommodate errors of the archer, whereas weaker arrows will behave more erratically on release and are less controllable.

weight is hung from the middle of an arrow shaft. Stiffer arrows will bend less, weaker arrows bend more. Hence weaker arrows will have higher numbers, that is, 920 rather than 500 spine.

Draw length

Bizarrely, arrows are measured from the groove of the nock point to the end of the arrow shaft rather than to the tip of the point. The best way to check what length arrows you need is to measure your draw length. Put an elastic band onto a long arrow. Draw the bow back to your anchor point whilst a friend moves the elastic band to where the arrow meets the front of the bow. Do this a few times to make sure you have a regular position. This point will give you a good couple of inches clearance for your first set of arrows.

Material

Aluminium shafts are great for your first set of arrows since they are available in a

Sight on inside of the riser to reach distance.

The best arrow is stiff enough to take advantage of thrust from bowstring, yet light enough to ensure good flight and accuracy. Too stiff and it could hit the bow, too weak and lots of wiggle in flight creates wider groupings.

Most advanced archers spend a lot of time and money on working out the right arrows for them, but as a beginner do not worry too much. As long as the arrows are not too short then you will be able to shoot reasonably well.

Fletches

The arrow is steered in flight with fletches. These can be plastic vanes, spin wings or feathers which all come in a huge variety of shapes, sizes and colours. If you are a beginner archer then go for durable, cheap plastic vanes in colours you like – then just get on and shoot. The difference of fletch will not make nearly as much difference as your shooting skills. Testing out fletching can be time consuming and you need relatively consistent weather, so really it is best left to when you are shooting longer distances and have more experience.

You should be aware that fletches will fall off. A lot! Most clubs have a fletching jig and glue where you can re-fix your fletches in place.

How to fletch an arrow

Fix the arrow in the jig using the nock and locate the start position. Make sure you start with the cock vane each time. Put the vane to be attached into the holder and run a thin layer of fletching glue (not normal glue) down the strip of vane that will fix to the arrow. Do not worry if there is a lot of glue; it will not affect things too much. You will get better the more you do.

Make sure the vane is far enough away from the arrow end, so that your fingers will not touch them. Normally ¼in is fine. Press the vane tightly on to the arrow shaft and leave for about 30 seconds or a minute before moving on to the next. (It is quite time consuming.)

Points/Piles

Points come in metal and tungsten and are available in standard weights for your arrow shaft. Points are glued into the shaft of the arrow using hot melt, a semi-permanent glue.

How to glue points

It is very simple to insert points into the arrow shaft. You will need some hot melt, access to a hot flame and a pair of pliers.

- Firmly hold the point end with the pliers and place the shaft end over the hot flame for about ten seconds.
- When it is hot, but not too hot, smear the glue bar over the point on two sides (you do not need much glue).
- Then whilst the point and glue are still warm push the point into the arrow end. Make sure the arrow shaft goes all the way down before popping the arrow end into a cup of cold water to cool it off. Do not push the arrow shaft down on the point too heavily because you can split the arrow end.
- Once the arrow has cooled take it out of the water and pick off the excess glue. You need very little glue really, so do not overload. If you find when pulling your arrows out of the boss the points stay in there you need to put a little more glue on next time.

How to remove points

- To take points out of an arrow shaft, heat the point over a hot flame to melt the glue. Be careful that the arrow shaft is not over the heat as you will damage it.
- Use a pair of pliers to ease out the point, which should release with ease. If not, add a little more heat until it pulls straight out. Do not wiggle the point as you can weaken or even split the arrow shaft end.

Nocks

Nocks come in just a few different sizes,

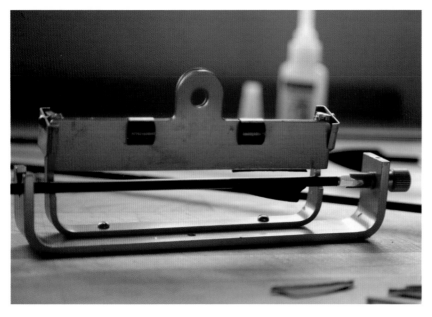

Fletching jig.

Nock test.

but in every colour imaginable. Choose a colour that can be seen in the target from afar. Fluorescent colours are excellent, but also very popular, so you might find yours are not quite so clear to detect on a boss as you might think.

A nock should clip onto the string neither too tightly nor too loosely. A loose fit can result in the arrow slipping off the string at full draw and causing a dry fire. A too-tight nock can cause erratic

release and send your arrow way off aim.

Nock test

Point your bow to the ground and nock your arrow onto the string so it hangs freely. Now gently tap the string. The arrow should drop off the string. If the arrow stays fast, then your nock is too small for your string size. If the arrow does not stay on the string by its own accord, then your string is too thin and you should use a smaller diameter.

Points over a flame.

PERSONAL TIP

Be warned, I shot an arrow with a nock too tight during an indoor shoot, and at 20 yards my arrow flew right across to the adjacent boss.

Protective gear

Bracer

The best bracer is one that protects your arm and keeps your clothing out of the way. Make sure it is not catching the string – the thinner the better.

> **PERSONAL TIP**
>
> Le Bruent, made from carbon, is the thinnest bracer I have found on the market. It is also moulded to fit the curve of your arm, so is great in summer with bare arms.

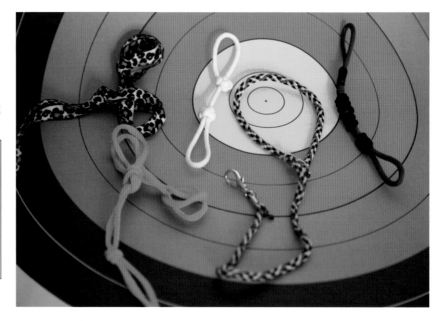

Slings.

Sling

A sling is there to stop the bow falling to the ground once it has been shot, because an archer does not actually hold their bow, but rests it within their hand. There are bow slings, wrist slings and finger slings. A finger sling is the most reliable and can be changed to suit your finger and hand size perfectly. The wrist sling and bow sling can both slip out of place, which unfortunately allows the bow to move forward an excessive amount on release; this can induce a habit to grab the bow.

The sling should fit on the first finger and the thumb. The length of the material between the finger and thumb should be just enough to catch the bow when it releases from your hand, but not too much so the bow drops or feels insecure; otherwise a catching habit

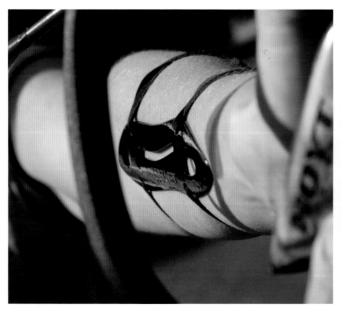

Bracer.

Finger sling shooting.

might develop. A good guide is about 1½in. Some archers use the middle finger and thumb, but this creates a longer string between the fingers and means the bow hand can turn inwards on shooting, thus inducing torque. A shoelace makes the best finger sling. You can change the length to suit yourself and change the colour when you like. And you will never have to worry if you accidentally lose your sling – there will always be an option to steal someone's shoelaces on the line!

How to tie a finger sling

Tabs.

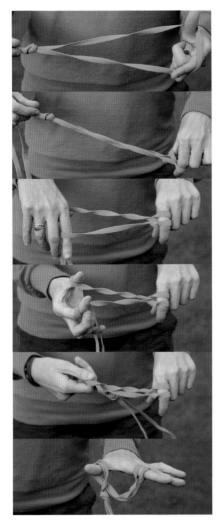

Finger sling tying.

Tab

A tab is very important to protect your fingers. Hands come in all sizes and so do tabs. The tab should cover your fingertips at full draw. The required thickness of protection is very much a comfort thing. The string should never hurt your fingers. If it does then add another layer of protection; or if you find the tips of your fingers are stinging on release then you need longer cover or a larger size.

Most tab faces are leather, but there are also other popular synthetic backings. There are many copies of the more expensive tabs on the market so do shop around for good prices. Some tabs are more angled than others, some come with finger hooks, shelf adjustability and variable spacers.

The best tab is one that helps align your hand with your jawbone at full draw. New archers are sometimes encouraged to get platform tabs, which are useful because you can feel the plastic platform, but this tab can work against the correct placement of your draw hand onto your jawline and can encourage a placement of the head onto the tab, rather than the hands coming into the correct position and finding the jawline.

Chestguard

The best chest guard is a flat, smooth surface. You can adapt your own and insert or sew material onto it. Some chest

Chestguard.

*Artebo
chestguard.*

guards are meshed, which can catch the string, especially when they become worn. Artebo have introduced a slip-on shoulder chest guard that helps keep all shoulder material out of the way and enables a choice of tops to be worn underneath it, giving a more snug fit than many over-the-counter guards.

Other accessories

Quiver

The quiver really has no effect on your shooting, so you can go wild.

There are two designs, the target design and the field design, which has a different angle and is preferred by some shooters.

Travelling kit

If you venture into competitive archery then you will most probably need a decent travelling bow case, a tent to protect yourself against the weather on long shoot days and a spotting scope to spot your arrows at the long distances.

Travelling bow case

Bow cases come in all shapes and sizes so it is really a choice of practicality. Will you be travelling to the archery field by car or on the bus? The backpacks are practical and popular for most people using public transport, whereas the hard cases are very protective but a little more cumbersome.

Spotting scope

Good optics are expensive, so finding a suitable scope is a little more tricky. What you want is a scope that allows in enough light for clarity and has enough distance to give you the detail of arrows on a target. You will find the cheaper scopes are usually larger in size so sometimes impractical to transport around, but the smaller scopes are incredibly expensive, even secondhand.

Tent

Any tent will suffice. Small, single units are quite practical since they are easy to put up, transport around and are keenly priced.

Tents.

CHAPTER 3

MAKING TECHNICAL ADJUSTMENTS

A shop will usually set up your newly bought bow for you, but you will benefit from knowing the basics, especially if you are purchasing secondhand equipment. Manufacturers' guidelines usually come with the bow or can be found on their website.

Bow adjustments

Limb alignment

You need the string to run through the centre of the bow. Rest the bow on the back of a chair (it helps if you have a long rod at this point – if not, try to borrow one) and stand directly behind it. Align the string with the boltholes on the riser so you can check that the string is running centrally through top and bottom limbs. Beiter limb gauges can be used to help with this. Your club will usually have a set. If the string is not in line with both bolts, you will have to make limb adjustments following the manufacturer's guidelines. This requires loosening the limb bolts and altering the limb alignment.

Tiller

Tiller is the term used to describe the relative bend of both limbs. The bow string is not pulled from the centre; since there is one finger above the arrow and two fingers under, this creates an uneven force toward the top of the bow. Tiller enables you to even out the disparity and make the force equal on both limbs so the limbs work together to produce a bow at its most efficient.

Measuring the tiller
To work out the tiller of your bow you

Limb alignment.

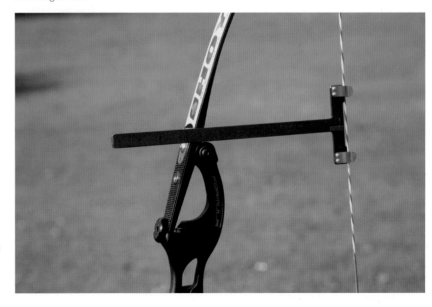

Tiller measurement.

take two measurements using your bow square: the first from the string and top limb, and the second from the string and the bottom limb. Positive tiller is when the distance from the string to the upper limb is greater than the distance between the string and the bottom limb; negative tiller is when the lower distance is greater; and zero tiller is when both measurements are equal.

Tiller goes through trends. As you gain experience, do play around and test things out, but for now check your bow manufacturer's guidelines, since this is the best setting to start with.

Changing tiller

Changing the tiller requires a loosening of the limb bolts and adding turns in or out. Unstring the bow. Undo the limb bolts; this usually involves a main bolt and an unlocking tiller bolt. To increase tiller add turns to the bottom limb bolt, then minus the same number of turns from the top limb bolt. Lock the bolts and restring the bow. Be careful, these are the same bolts that change your poundage! How many turns you need varies on the type of limb and riser combination, but normally working off quarter or half turns is enough. Do make sure you do not wind your bolts too far out. There should be enough bolt still in the limb at all times. And remember, tiller will also affect your nocking point so this may need changing too.

Arrow set correctly from above.

Arrow set correctly from below.

Arrow rest and button

The arrow rest should be set so your arrows lie central on the button and the arm supports the arrow, but does not jut out beyond the arrow shaft since this can catch the arrow and cause erratic arrow flight. Screw the button into the bow. We will set this later.

Brace height

Set the brace height to a position within the recommendation from the bow manufacturer. ILF fittings are normally between 8.25 and 9.5, whereas some of the latest bows, or bows with much more curve to their limbs such as Border Hex

Arrow rest arm set wrongly from above.

5s, will recommend a much lower brace height.

Nock point

The best start is to use an adjustable nock point such as the small brass clips or use small pieces of electrical tape cut down to the width of 2–4mm. (It is best to wind the tape on the string in the opposite direction to how your fingers move off on release; otherwise your fingers unwind it off the string rather quickly.) There is a lot of talk about tuning with the exact same materials for the nock point that you will then shoot with, but doing it this way is fine for your very first bow tune.

How to set a nock point
Position the bow square on your string and the arrow rest, making sure it is clipped on the string with a 90 per

Correct start position for nock point.

cent angle. Position the bottom of your nocking point about 5mm above the square. Clip on an arrow or a nock and fix your top nock so that it is just above the nock and a lower nock just underneath. You want a tight fit that has a tiny bit of give, but not too much. Always use a top and bottom nock as otherwise the fingers may push the arrow high or low on release. When you are happy with your final nock point position, you can put on an

actual nock point that will be semi-permanent. The easiest way to fix a nock point in place is to use dental floss.

Fixing a floss nock point
Tie the floss onto the string at the point where the top of your bottom nock point should be. Make sure it is tight. Take one end of the floss and hold it close to the string in a loop, whilst winding the other end around both the

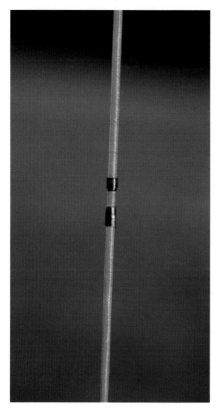

Taped on nock point.

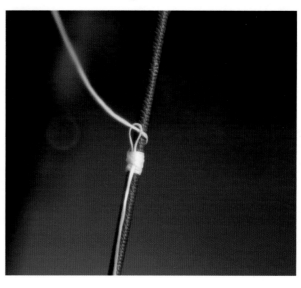

Fixing on floss point.

string and the held piece of floss. Make about 8 turns, keeping the floss tight together on each wind. Now put the single end of floss through the loop and pull very tight. Use a slip knot to tie it off. Cut the floss short and with a lighter burn the loose ends back to the main knot so it fuses together. Give it a pinch to make sure. Now place your arrow onto the string and mark the top of the nock. Repeat the process. When you are done dab a tiny amount of fletch glue or superglue on top of both nock points. Superglue will go hard and break off in the future whereas arrow glue will wear off. If this happens, just add a little more glue again, before the knots come undone. (Inevitably this will always happen at a competition!)

Centre shot and arrow alignment

Centre shot is the set-up that makes the arrow shoot straight. Ironically,

the whole point of setting up the centre shot is to point the arrow off centre to take into account the Archer's Paradox (see Chapter. 2) or the effect the fingers have on the bow string.

To do this, rest the bow on the back of a chair with an arrow in place on the arrow rest. Stand behind the bow. Centre up the string with the riser bolts, and look to see where the very tip of your arrow is. You want it to be just left of the string. Screw your button in or out until the arrow shaft just shows to the left of the string. Placing a white piece of paper underneath the arrow can help distinguish the placement.

Set sight

You need the sight bar setting at a point that is low enough for you to reach your furthest distance (70m), and high enough to accommodate the

nearest distance (18m). You can of course bring the sight right in, or even turn it backwards, for the furthest distance.

Set the sight pin so it is directly down the centre of the string and over the arrow. It is important to make sure the actual sight block is vertically aligned; otherwise you may find you have to move your windage at every change of distance. To check this, set the sight pin so it is on the string while the bow is at rest, and move the sight block to the top of the sight bar. Now move the sight bar down, checking that the sight pin stays central. If it does not, then loosen the block and correct it before re-tightening.

Clicker

A clicker is there to help you come to the exact same draw length every time you shoot. It is not there to tell you when to shoot. A clicker is mounted beneath the sight bracket, so that as the arrow tip pulls past the clicker arm, the arm clicks onto the plate making a snap sound. This is not a signal to shoot, but it should – if it is set correctly – click at the same time as you release.

There are adjustable clickers and extension plates to fit onto your bow. Clickers do come with different screw sizes so again check the bow manufacturer website for what suits your bow. The clicker should not be too tight to the arrow as it can push against the arrow and cause interference. Clickers can often get caught or come loose when putting your bow together, so it is a good idea to put a piece of sticky tape on the clicker plate and mark where your clicker sits. This way you can check on settings when you put your bow together or mid-shoot. As a beginner your draw length will change as your form develops, so at this stage do not worry about a clicker at all yet.

Centre point.

Stabilizer system

The balance of your bow is important to aid your steadiness in aiming. You do not want a bow too heavy or too light. Stabilizer systems help you weight the bow to shoot your style. These really come into play at the longer distances, so again, is something you should explore once you have been shooting for a little while.

Tuning

The most important thing for a beginner is to be able to achieve consistent grouping, improve your form whilst having fun. A basic tune can make sure that your equipment is shooting consistently, but really, as a beginner there will be a lot of variation every time you shoot, so a tune on one day may produce different results the following week so do not get too hung up tuning. Fine tuning is really for when you are shooting all your arrows in the red at your second furthest competitive distance.

Brace height tune

Choose a near distance that you can shoot an adequate group of arrows at, say 18m. Shoot some arrows to warm up first, then every six arrows or so increase the brace height. Just undo your string and add in three twists then put it back on your bow and shoot. Continue doing this until you find the quietest sound of your bow or until your arrows group tightly. This is often at the top or bottom end of the recommended brace height range. When you begin shooting the quietness of a bow is quite difficult to detect; a poor release can twang the string, other people may be chatting or you are just not sure what is loud and what is not. If this is the case do not worry. Try to choose the setting that gave you the best group on the target. These tests are not critical.

Bare shafts

Bare shaft tuning is the most common way to get a basic tune of your arrows.

Bare shaft showing high nock point.

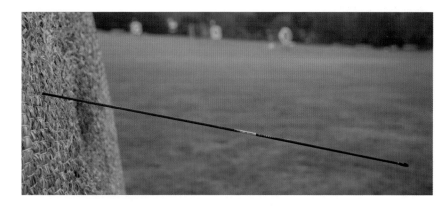

Bare shaft showing low nock point.

Bare shaft showing correct position.

However, even if you cannot get a great match do not despair. Fletched arrows can shoot and group well even if they are not perfectly tuned. Choose a calm day or shoot indoors, because wind and rain will affect the results.

Fletch five arrows and leave three unfletched (called bare shafts). A duff arrow will complicate matters, so having three unfletched hopefully helps clarify the outcome quickly. Since there are no fletches to stabilize the arrow, the bare shaft will show the true flight path of the arrow. If your arrows are flying well without fletches, when they are fletched they will form even tighter groups. Many archers suggest putting the same weight on the bare shafts by adding tape in place of the fletches of the same weight. This is not necessary. The aerodynamics of tape at the back of the arrow will create a false tune. Keep the arrow bare.

Nock point set-up

The first thing is to set the correct position of your nock. Place a bare shaft into the bow and stand about four feet directly in front of a boss. When you feel you have a very straight line of the arrow to the target, then release your arrow. Get a fellow archer to check that your arrow is horizontal on release. Take a look at your arrow. If the nock of the arrow is high then your nock point is too high. If your nock is low then your nock point is too low. (Bear in mind that a straw boss can sometimes alter the angle of the arrow as it enters the boss, so do this a few times to check.) Adjust your nock point by 1 or 2mm up or down depending on the result, until the arrow ends up straight with the nock point directly behind.

Move back to about 18m and shoot again. Shoot the bare shafts randomly with the fletched arrows. Do not leave them to last when you might be tiring. Once again check if the bare shafts fly high or low in relation to your fletched group, and correct accordingly until they are flying at the same height as your fletched group. It is helpful at this point to make a precise mark or stick a line of electrical tape on your bow square, so

Bare shafts shooting correctly.

Bare shaft shooting weak.

Bare shafts shooting stiff.

Adjustments to try

To make the arrow shoot stiffer

- Decrease brace height (which will change the nock position).
- Decrease point weight.
- Add weight to nock end.
- Increase string strands.
- Shorten arrow shaft.
- Decrease bow weight.

If these are no good then you will need to choose a stiffer shaft of arrow or weaker limbs. Obviously, there are limitations here. For example, increasing weight on the bow may mean it is too heavy for you, so try the simplest first.

To make the arrow shoot weaker

- Increase brace height.
- Increase point weight.
- Decrease string strands.
- Increase bow weight.

If these do not help then you will need to choose a weaker shaft of arrow or stronger limbs.

Relax and work on your form

When you are just starting out if you can get your fletched arrows to shoot reasonably well, even if your bare shafts do not fly in the same place, then stick with this tune. Sometimes, if you concentrate too intensely on your bow set-up at this early stage it can take your attention off improving form, which is really where good shooting originates from. It can also create insecurity in your equipment, and once you lose faith in your bow you will soon become disheartened. However, if you enjoy shooting and a little bit of tuning now and again, you will find you progress much more quickly.

you know where your nock point is for future reference.

Bare shaft tuning (for right-handed archers)

Shoot all your arrows. Now look at the horizontal relationship of your fletched arrows and the bare shafts. Shoot two or three times to check patterns are repeating. You want all the arrows to group together. If the bare shafts are hitting to the left of the group it means the arrows are flying stiff, without much bend. Increase the pressure on your button by a quarter or half a turn. If the bare shafts are hitting to the right of the group it means the arrows are flying weak and bending a little too much, then soften the button by the same.

Changing the button pressure

Use the allen keys provided and undo the grub screws. Be careful, they can easily be overtightened or fall out and

HANDY HINT

Righty tighty! Simple and stupid, but this is how I always remember which way to turn the button to make it stiffer.

are extremely difficult to find in long grass. You change the actual button pressure by undoing the grub screw furthest from the riser, inserting the allen key into the end of the button and turning it right or left. Turning it clockwise, or right, increases the pressure by pushing down on the small spring inside the button, whereas turning it anticlockwise, or left, decreases the pressure and makes the button softer. Quarter or half turns are advisable, but make a note of how many turns you make in case you have to go backwards. Generally, a button that feels soft like a pen push-in top is about right. A soft button will be more forgiving than a very stiff button.

Smiles on the line.

PART II
THE TECHNICAL SKILLS

CHAPTER 4

BASIC SHOOTING TECHNIQUE

The aim of target archery is simple: to hit the gold again and again. However, the task is surprisingly difficult. Archery is a sport of repetition. The form you build needs to be repeatable, shot after shot as you try to shoot an arrow in the same place time and time again.

Grouping is a visual indication that you are repeating an action. Archery is all about learning to group. You can change where the group land, by moving your sight, but it is really only form and technique that will give you those elusive groups to start with. Consequently, your fundamental form needs to be comfortable and natural to give you the stability and consistency you need for successful shooting.

Take up your position

Once your bow is ready, prepare yourself. Put on your chest guard, bracer and finger sling.

Stance

Your stance forms the basis of your technique, and posture provides the foundation of your shot. The placement of your feet affects the direction of the body and the direction of aiming, so it is crucial to get right. There are two set positions: the square stance and the open stance.

Square stance.

The square, or closed, stance is when the feet are parallel to the target on either side of the shooting line. The width of your stance depends on your physique, but for most people the natural alignment of the body is to place your feet under your shoulders to make your body as stable as possible; otherwise you introduce a lean as you begin to draw the bow.

Shooting shot.

Open stance.

Flat shoes are best because they allow correct placement of weight on your feet. Running shoes often have raised heels and can push the centre onto the balls of the feet.

Nocking an arrow

Take up the bow and fix on your finger sling. Take an arrow and place it on the arrow rest before sliding it back to nock onto the string. Make sure it clips on securely.

The open stance is when the feet are placed so that the hips are more open to the target. This introduces a twist to the lower torso to bring the top into alignment. Although more stable in windy conditions it is more difficult to maintain; you are likely to lose your line or find your back hollowing out as you tire. The square stance is the best starting position, although wider archers sometimes find they need an open stance to get enough string clearance.

Some coaches advocate that the back foot should be parallel to the shooting line and the forward foot pointing toward the target in a V stance, but I find this creates tension on the front knee joint, or sometimes in the leg–hip joint. The Korean school of thought is that 60 per cent of your weight should be on the front of the foot and 40 per cent on the heels. Do not lock your knees but maintain a relaxed position with your centre of gravity pointing directly between your two feet.

Nocking an arrow.

Finger placement

Hook your fingers around the string so it nestles into the first bend of the fingers. You are first taught to shoot using the barebow style, which is three fingers underneath the arrow and drawing back to your eye to aim using the end of the arrow.

Once this is mastered you will move on to using a sight and the Olympic style of anchoring under your chin. Place the index finger above the arrow and the other two underneath. The fingers should fit naturally around the string, and should not pinch the arrow or clench the string, or be held in too deep a hook. If the arrow keeps falling off as you draw the bow it is usually because your first and second fingers are pinching the string.

Finger placement on string.

Head

Set your head position. Start off by looking ahead with your shoulders set straight; then in one fluid movement turn your head to address the target.

Set your head position.

Address the target.

Pre-draw

Take up a little tension on the string and let your hand settle naturally into the grip. Do not take hold of the bow. At no point should you actually grip the riser. Gripping will torque the bow and interfere with the bow's forward motion, so try to avoid it from the start. Instead, think of just using the string tension to keep the bow nestled in your hand. If you feel you are grabbing the grip widen your fingers a little so the handle anchors into your hand. The side of the grip should be cushioned in your lifeline. The fingers should be relaxed rather than curled around the handle. This stage is important to get right, because once the bow is drawn your muscles become taut which makes changing technique much more difficult to do.

The stages of shooting

Although the next stages of raise, draw, anchor, aim and release are broken down into their separate elements, what you are trying to do is to create one fluid movement. Some coaches tell the archer to sing as they draw the bow to help instil a sense of rhythm and regularity; you will soon know if you are drawing too fast or slow when you reach your anchor at a different point in your chosen song.

Raise

Relax your forearms. You have to repeat this movement time after time so remain as relaxed as possible. Rotate the elbow down and away. It is quite a difficult thing to do at first, but will become more natural as time progresses. This helps the shoulder remain low and encourages the right muscles to work correctly. Focus on the target as you raise both arms together bringing the bow to about nose height so it is aligned with the target. There should be a slight bend in your front arm. If the bow arm is too straight the elbow tends

Pre draw.

HANDY HINT

As you draw the bow the sight drops, so use gravity to help you settle onto the gold. If you start the draw on the gold you will find your sight will settle low and you will have to raise the bow to get back there, which is a much more difficult feat to accomplish. Begin your draw with your sight at 12 o'clock on the target.

ABOVE: Bring the bow to about nose height.

LEFT: The draw is an equal force of push and pull.

to lock. Your sight should be about 12 o'clock on the target toward the top in the black.

Draw

Now draw the string back toward your face whilst also reaching forward with your bow arm. Try to keep both hands relaxed by letting your fingers take up the weight without much thought and use your back muscles rather than your arm. These muscles are bigger and stronger. With your front arm, imagine trying to reach forward to try to touch something that is just out of reach. The draw should be an equal force of both push and pull. Often, as a beginner it seems you are pulling much more than pushing, mainly because you are not aware of the work your front arm is doing. Endeavour to draw with one continuous movement since stop and start is more difficult to control. Think of your arm as a chain, drawing back toward your ear, pulling your hand backwards. You're aiming to get the power of force behind the arrow so that when it is released it flies straight. If the force is on the arm this means the force is on an angle and so sends the arrow off to one side or the other.

The draw should come from the centre of the body, which should remain vertical. It's natural to lean away from a lifted weight, but try not to lean back. If a line were drawn it should drop down through the head, the hips and the centre part of the ankles. Draw back until the string touches the centre of your chin and the centre of your nose. This is a good reference point that is simple to repeat. Do try to keep the bow vertical too. A bow can be shot on a cant, but it is more difficult to achieve consistent arrow placement. Mostly you'll find the arrows fly in the direction of the lean. There are a lot of pointers to think of, but the contour of the bow is designed to work with the shape of the body, (thousands of years of design!) so you'll find a lot of these pointers just sort of fall into place! As you do it time

The body remains vertical with no lean.

Coming to anchor – 1.

Coming to anchor – 2.

A good tight anchor.

Think of your arm as a chain pulling backwards.

The string touches the centre of the nose and the chin.

and time again you'll become more aware of each stage and hopefully can take more control of each component.

Anchor

The anchor is really your rear sight and plays a major part in aiming. A good anchor should securely fix the draw hand under the chin and should come to the same position every single time. Archery is about trying to get as many constants as possible so that once they are all aligned you know you are in the best position to achieve the same result again and again.

At the anchor point the top of the forefinger should fix under the jawbone on the bone line. The tendency is to rest the chin on the hand by moving your head to the hand, whereas what you really need to do is to bring your hand to your head. Push your hand right into the side of your jawline so you get a really deep anchor. The closer the contact of hand and finger to neck and chin can be achieved, the more solid the anchor will be. It will never be too tight!

The thumb should be relaxed, but kept inside the tab. (Some archers shoot with their thumb atop the tab, but sometimes the thumb can unknowingly rise up or send tension into the hand causing poor releases, especially when tired, tense or under pressure such as in competition.)

The Asian archers usually have a centre anchor to the centre of their nose and chin, whereas the USA and many Europeans draw to the centre of the nose, but with the string a little off-centre to the outside of the mouth which is called a side anchor. This is often

String picture.

determined by the shape of your face and your overall physique. Try to go with what comes naturally.

String picture

As the string is drawn back to your face it forms a single blurred line. This is your string picture. Normally, it comes to a natural constant place, such as the righthand side of your sight pin or bow window. Shoot a few times and see where it ends up. Try to keep the blur in the

same place. This will help keep your bow straight and help stop right and left shots. Make sure too, that it does not change during the anchor stage. Sometimes if you turn your hand or grip your fingers you can alter the alignment just prior to release. This can also come from a wrongly sized tab twisting in your hand as you draw back.

Aiming

As you come to anchor you also need to start aiming. Oh, so many things to think about! Aiming is actually something you will find comes naturally.

It is impossible to hold a sight pin steadfast on a target at 70m or 90m, so bizarrely aiming is not about aiming at all, but about bringing the body to point of a stillness that enables a controlled release.

HANDY HINT

Moving the head is a common tendency you should try to avoid early on. Counter-productive habits include placing the head on to the anchor hand, leaning the head away as you draw the string to your face, stretching the neck forward or using the lips to kiss the string rather than bringing the string to the nose. Our bodies and brains always try to go for the least demanding option!

You can keep both eyes open or use your dominant eye. Some people find they lose focus or see two targets with both eyes. Many archers narrow their eyes until their dominant eye takes over the aiming toward the end of the shot.

Full draw

You will reach the full draw position when your body has come into balance and is ready to release the arrow. Drawing a bow requires the effort of muscle, but once in position the success shot depends on bone on bone alignment. Keeping shoulders even, your weight balanced over your feet and your back straight should enable you to bring your draw elbow into alignment and enable you to achieve a good force line at full draw. The force line is an imaginary line that runs from the bow hand and the back elbow. If all the force is directly behind the arrow then the arrow's trajectory will be straight and true to the point of aim.

Having a good posture in this position is a crucial part of shooting good scores. The front shoulder should be low. The back should not be hollowed and the chest should not stick out. When it works well you should have the feeling of what is called Being in the Bow: existing between the two forces of the push and pull.

Release

You cannot actually control the release of the hand. Instead, you have to control everything around it. The Koreans teach that the release is a reaction, not an action. Try to think about the expansion between the push and pull of your arms rather than the release of the arrow.

It is easier to concentrate on the follow-through, which enables the release to become automatic. Concentrate on taking your elbow just that little bit further back as you push that little bit forward. Good release really is just allowing the string to slip out and around the fingers at the right moment. However, the fingers should not open. It should look as though nothing has changed.

The Queen's wave

If you focus on the release it becomes a challenge to do it right. Your mind moves to your hand, which usually results in a forward release where you clutch the string on release or move your hand forward, flicking the fingers out of the way with an exaggerated movement called the Queen's wave.

Follow-through

As the string is released, the hand should follow back in the same trajectory. Your elbow and hand should move along the same line with the finger tracing the neck. Your draw hand should end up by the ear rather than around the back of your neck or atop your shoulder. Too far back usually means the hand is flicking out around the string.

After release the bow should jump forward with the propulsion. Advanced archers often appear as though they are actually throwing the bow forward, whereas it is merely the powerful push of the archer that is causing this reaction.

A well-executed follow-through prevents many mistakes, and a good release means a minimal interference with the string to give a clean arrow flight.

LEFT: *Full draw..*

BELOW RIGHT: *Follow through*

LEFT: The bow moves forward on release.

BELOW: A well executed follow-through, showing the bow being propelled out of the hand.

Getting it right

If you have a square stance you will hopefully find that as the bow jumps forward it will rotate so that the lower limb hits your front leg. This is a good indicator that your line of release is straight. If you have an open stance the bow will swing up past your nose instead. Repeated feedback like this is a great help in confirming the uniformity of each shot.

Learning to be an archer is rather like becoming a ballerina or a concert pianist. Musicians and dancers practise the basics of their technique before putting it all together in a single, fluid performance. In the same way, an archer concentrates on different elements of their shot cycle until hopefully, without too much thought, they are able to repeat their performance time after time. From there on in, the finessing can begin.

CHAPTER 5

THE ARCHERY FIELD

Beginning to shoot at targets

Once you have completed your beginner's course and have joined a club you will no longer be limited to group shooting, although all junior archers do need to be under supervision of an adult at all times.

Distances

Practise the distances you are comfortable with. Remember to follow the arrow: if the arrows are low, then lower your sight. If the arrows go left, then move your windage left and vice versa.

Use a small notebook to mark down your sight mark on the sight bar for each distance. It sometimes takes a good few arrows to find the correct setting, so noting it down helps you replicate your actions when you next come to shoot that distance. Note the windage too. It is helpful to make a note of the weather too, since weather affects the arrow flight. That way you learn to see the difference a rainy day can make to your sight marks.

When you can group comfortably or your arrows are landing in the red then increase your distance. Build up gradually.

Finding your arrows

When you do move distance move your sight incrementally, since shooting low arrows means they are much easier to find than sending them way off over the top of the boss. If you do miss the boss start to look within about a twenty-yard radius. Unless the arrow

Target faces on shoot field.

clipped the boss, which can send it shooting off on an odd angle, you should be able to find your arrow. Most clubs have metal detectors for retrieving lost arrows. Be warned though, that arrows can bury deep in soft wet grass or can go skimming across very hard or frozen ground to end up quite a distance from the target.

Soon you will progress onto shooting rounds.

Rounds

In archery a round is the name given to a set number of arrows shot at a set distance. There are lots of different rounds that embrace all abilities. These set rounds provide a regulated method that enables you to draw score comparison with similar shooters as well as achieve certain classifications in your shooting. Scoring at set rounds can also help you recognize your progression as your practice falls into place.

Rules for rounds

All rounds are shot according to Archery GB, commonly referred to as GNAS, rules or the European equivalent of World Archery (WA) or FITA. There are four main sizes of paper faces used at different distances: 122cm and 80cm for outdoors and 60cm and 40cm for indoors.

Archery GB
Outdoor Archery GB rounds are always shot using big faces at imperial distances, and are scored using the five-zone scoring method which uses the colours for scoring: yellow scores 9 points, red 7, blue 5, black 3 and white only 1. The top score of six arrows is 54. Common rounds shot are the York, Hereford, Bristol I–V.

WA
WA or FITA rounds are shot at metric distances and, although the same paper face is used, inner scoring is counted. The inner ring in the gold scores 10 points whereas the outer ring in the gold scores 9. Likewise, the inner red scores 8, but the outer red a 7 and so on down to the outer white, netting you 1 point only. There is also a small ring right in the centre of the gold inside the inner ring. If you hit this you score a 10, but mark it as an X. If two competitors end a competition with identical scores the one with the most Xs is declared the winner. (The X is also called the Spider.)

The top score from one end of a FITA round is 60 points. Popular metric rounds are the full FITA now called the WA 1440, WA 70, the Short Metric and Metrics I–V.

Indoor rounds, such as the Portsmouth, are shot at 20yd, whereas the WA is shot at their named distance in metres such as WA 25 shot at 25m or WA 18 shot at 18m.

Ten-zone scoring.

Sighters

In every round an archer shoots the longest distance first after a number of sighters, which are a number of arrows to help check your sight mark. Sighters are given for the furthest distance only, which means you need to know your sight marks for the other distances being shot (if not, don't expect great scores!).

Score sheet

A score sheet shows the individual arrow score. Each set of shot arrows is called an end and is totalled on the sheet. There is also the total of the dozen. Individual arrow scores are scored from the highest scoring arrow through to the lowest and are called out in threes, for example 9, 7, 5 – 5, 5, 2. The hits are the number of scoring arrows per dozen and the golds are the number of tens shot (not nines). The righthand total is the running total and is incremental. Once the arrow is removed the actual arrow score cannot be altered, but the addition can be changed.

Awards

There are many awards you can achieve in archery, from club classifications to world-recognition. Traditionally, these come in the form of badges that most people pin on their quiver, hat or archery bag.

Classification

Every round has a set score for certain classifications, which takes into account age, gender and bow style of the shooter.

Competition shooting.

Scoring by target.

Shooting rounds for classification is greatly enjoyable. It gives you a sense of purpose and helps give you something to aim for as you practise. To gain a classification you must have the actual scores witnessed by another archer, so it is a good way to hook up with other archers of similar ability. You must shoot at least three rounds to gain ranking, which you then submit to your club's records officer who will award you your badge of achievement. Wear it with pride!

First, second, third class and Bowman classifications can all be achieved by shooting at your club ground.

To qualify for Master, Junior Master, Grandmaster Bowman or Junior Grand Master Bowman, however, an archer must submit scores from a record status shoot which is more stringently run than club shoots. Averaged out, a Bowman accounts for the top 15 per cent of shooters, a Master Bowman the top 2 per cent and a Grandmaster the top 1 per cent.

Score sheet.

Other awards

There are other awards bestowed for scores at set distances or set rounds, such as the Rose awards, WA Star (once called FITA Stars) and the 252 scheme, with the most coveted badge of all being the All Gold End, presented for all six arrows in the gold at the longest distance of shooting.

Handicap

Archery GB produce tables that give set handicaps for any score in any round, split across outdoor and indoor. Handicaps are not related to anything other than the physical score of a round, but they can enable archers of different abilities to compete on an equal footing. The lower the handicap, the better the archer.

The handicap system also enables archers to compare scores across different rounds they are shooting. Your handicap can go up and down and is normally calculated at the end of each season with your three highest scores being rounded up to give you an average handicap. There is a great little website called Archer's Mate which calculates your handicap for you, so you can compare your shooting after each shot round.

Shooting line etiquette

Arrows

Shoot six arrows at a time, unless you are alone or the shooters agree to shoot more or less arrows. Generally it is polite to try to average your time to the time everyone else is shooting so no one is waiting a long time before collecting. (The amount of arrows shot is called an end.)

Rather than just pulling your own arrows from the target, do ask other archers if they are happy for you to pull theirs. Sometimes archers prefer to pull their own arrows, if they are shooting wooden shafts or very expensive arrows.

Target

When joining other archers on a target it is polite to ask if it is all right with them. Usually they welcome the company, but sometimes an archer might be tuning or changing distance at the next end and so can let you know this.

For safety's sake if you want to move a boss to a different distance, do let people on the line know in advance, just in case they do not

Pin badges on quiver.

Shoot line.

notice you are behind a boss and begin shooting.

If an archer leaves their bow in front of a target it usually means they are shooting that distance and have gone for a rest break. By all means shoot that distance, but do not move the boss to a different distance without asking them first.

Talking on the line

Feel free to chat a little on the line, but be considerate to other archers since some prefer to shoot in relative quiet. Do not make comments on other people's scores or start comparing scores out loud, which can be very off-putting to other archers.

Most archers are happy to offer help or advice if asked, but be careful you do not become a persistent bother every time you show up, as it can become tiresome to other archers who just want to practise their own form.

Helping out

Do help other archers search for lost arrows. Rather than holding up the shooting line searching for an arrow, look after each end instead if possible – most times other archers will help, which makes a find much quicker.

Do help in setting up or putting away bosses if needed. Even if you cannot roll a boss, offering to collect up pegs and so on is always welcome.

PART III

TACTICS

CHAPTER 6

BUILDING THE BEST FORM

Once you have mastered the initial technique of shooting then you can begin to build form. The secret is in the fluidity and efficiency of motion. Precision does not come from holding the sight pin steady on the gold – in fact, this is truly impossible, especially at the longer distances. Instead, the goal is on creating a rhythm that enables exactness and accuracy. When you watch great archers the process looks seamless, elegant, even at times robotic; Park Sung-Hyun has a shot rhythm that is almost perfectly replicated to the millisecond on every shot, but every one of these archers is at work on controlling every minute aspect of their form. This is commonly referred to as 'feeling the shot'.

What to work on

Stance

As shooting improves you can vary your posture until you find your natural point of aim. Open or close your stance to find the most comfortable position. Practise drawing your bow on the line with your eyes closed. Bring up your bow, draw back and then open your eyes and see where you are pointing. If you are right to the target open your stance a little more, if left, try to close your stance a little. Repeat this a few times to make sure it is correct for you.

If it is a windy day you may be more naturally inclined to adopt a more open stance that will feel oddly uncomfortable on a calm day. Angling your feet 10 per cent outwards should give you the most stability.

Grip

It is natural for us to hold things with our hands, so it can be easy to grip the grip. (It should not really be called a grip!) The pre-draw should hopefully encourage your hand to

On the line.

10 per cent foot square stance.

PERSONAL TIP

I had a terrible habit of gripping the bow with a lot of tenseness in my fingers. Even when I thought I was allowing the bow to fall free I found my thumb and finger were nipping the handle and torqueing the bow on every release.

To overcome this habit I used a very loose finger sling so I could make sure the bow dropped right away from my hand. But then, because my bow jumped out of my hand and swung oddly due to the loose sling I found I would then attempt to snatch the bow back — thereby developing a different bad habit!

Grip modified.

settle into a natural position without grabbing, but sometimes as you are concentrating on other things your fingers will start to wrap around the bow as you draw.

If the pressure point changes during the draw then the bow will torque and send the arrows left and right, even up and down, depending on how the pressure has changed. Other times, you can find you actually place your hand too far over into the grip. Remember, the angle of the grip should run down your lifeline. Marking the bow handle with sticky tape can help with placement. You can also quickly check at any time of the draw that your hand has not moved over.

Do try out grips, since there are a lot of variables out there. Many shooters adapt their grips with a putty material that they mould to suit their hand, but it is best to become quite experienced before doing this.

HANDY HINT

Many archers like to put tennis grip on their handle because they find their handle can become sweaty in hot weather or indoors. I use climber's chalk on my palm, whereas Steve Hallard, who has competed in four Olympics, used to spray his hand with a well-known deodorant to stop the sweat affecting his grip.

Head position

Head movement can often cause problems or variation with string alignment during the draw. Your head moves so much in everyday life it is actually quite a feat to keep it still during the drawing of a bow. String alignment is related to your head position, so keeping your head straight will help maintain consistency. Drawing the string back to

Head position.

Draw hand.

String to nose.

the centre of your nose helps preserve this straightness. If the string is pulled to the right of your nose the arrows will fly left, and vice versa.

Finger position

The placement of fingers is important. The desirable weight on each finger is roughly 40 per cent top finger, 60 per cent index finger and 20 per cent for the third finger. Fluctuating pressures can cause the arrows to go high and low. The hold should be on the first bend of the fingers. If the string is on the pads of the fingers, then the string can sometimes slip and release early or deflect the string on release, whereas too deep a hold and the fingers tend to snatch the string and create a slow release or deflection. The first finger position should be the same for every archer, but between archers there is usually some variation on the other two fingers depending on the archer's hand size.

String alignment

String alignment helps eliminate left and right arrows. The position of the string should fall to the right of the sight pin or with the vertical of the bow window. Inconsistent string alignment will cause arrows to fly left and right of aim. If you can find a natural constant it will really help you shoot straight. As you draw back try to close your eyes as you come to full draw and then open them as you reach your anchor point. Where is the string position? Try it a few times and see if there is a consistent placement. Generally the best location depends on your head position and your posture as well as the type of riser you are shooting with.

Aiming

Many elements happen simultaneously in archery. Aiming is one. Eye focus should be on the point of aim rather than the

Draw elbow height.

PERSONAL TIP

Some archers advise circle on circle for the sight pin. I shoot with a pin, because without it I feel I am too casual in my aiming and the pin encourages me to seek the very centre of the gold.

---

sight pin. Maintaining motion is actually more relevant than aiming. The sight pin should feel as though it is floating freely as you come to anchor.

Draw elbow

The elbow position directly affects finger pressure. A high elbow usually means the ring finger is bearing most of the pressure with very little on the lower fingers, whereas a low elbow creates more pressure on the first finger causing the hand to open up and lift away from the string on release. A low elbow can also cause a soreness on the first finger joint. Some schools of thought advocate the elbow should be 3–6 degrees above the arrow, others believe your elbow can never be too high as long as your hand is tucked into your anchor position and you have good finger placement. Once again, an individual's physiology comes into play.

Back tension

As you come to anchor, there should be enough room in your back to allow for the final expansion that will take the arrow through the clicker. The anchor point helps eliminate up and down arrows. It should not really be a point of static, but a point of reference. Sometimes, archers draw right back so their shoulder blades have no room to expand through the last few millimetres of release.

Back tension.

Release and follow-through

A good release is worth practising early on. The elbow and shoulder should be used rather than the hand, which should remain relaxed. If your fingers are under tension then the hand is not relaxed and so you will clutch the string on release – you cannot open your fingers in time to get out of the way of the string.

If you imagine 'releasing' the string then you will transfer the thought onto the hand, causing the hands to give a forward release or a weak shot without proper follow-through. It is common to 'fake' the release where the hand actually lets go of the string but then moves backward into position.

The release often needs to be stronger than anticipated. We tend to soften up at this point as we wait for the arrow to be released. A forward release can also be caused by 'collapsing', when the shoulders relax prior to release. Do keep looking at your point of aim right until the arrow hits the target; otherwise you will find your bow arm drops and you can develop a habit of peeking to see where your arrow hits.

The Zen of archery, or the mental game

Archery is as much a mental game as physical. The Zen of archery is really when you are working in such a way that the body is occupied but the mind is free…but not too free. Your mind cannot be too occupied by the task in hand – that of shooting – but then neither can it be too far removed; thinking of what you are having for tea tonight. This is difficult to understand, achieve and practise.

Archery is greatly rewarding when you are shooting well, and incredibly frustrating when you are not. If you are to commit to this sport then you do need mental stamina to push through the low points.

Plateau

It is common to learn archery and then, as everything comes together and your body starts understanding its new requirements, you have a huge spurt of improvement. This is your first year.

The second year is tough, and many archers drop off at this point, as you reach a plateau. Improvement is slower. Scores

seem harder to reach. And you sometimes feel threatened by the new, enthusiastic beginners who seem to be shooting better than you.

The reality is that you are trying to aim the tip of a pencil to land 70m away. The premise surely is absurd. It is an impossible task – almost but not quite, because at times you can certainly do it.

Many times archers will shoot to their expectations. If you are shooting well, you suddenly feel out of your comfort zone and then collapse. Or if you are shooting badly, you often pull things together and end up hitting an average score. This is natural and normal. It takes time to build up your mental confidence and belief in yourself. That is why working on your end average will help you realize your real average.

Once you begin to think too much you can lose your rhythm. Try to maintain rhythm and routine because these will help anchor your style and form. Slowly, as you improve you should see your end average improve: 4 in the red at 60m rather than 3, or 5 in the yellow at 50m rather than 4.

Building confidence

Your confidence will come from your goals. If you expect too much and are unrealistic you will fight disappointment, whereas if you are realistic about what you can aim for in the short term you will fulfil each step and build confidence. A confident shooter shoots well. Making mistakes is common. It takes mental strength to come back from an obvious error. The more professional the competitor, the quicker they will bounce back from a bad arrow. This comes down purely to mental control: thinking about the next arrow rather than the last.

Focusing on the centre of the target, but not the score is difficult in a sport based on scoring. In competition everything is exaggerated. You cannot be too excited or too laid back. Racing adrenalin can affect your shot just as much as sluggishness. You cannot be distracted by external elements. This

Eyes remain on target after release. The bow rotates, sending the lower limb upwards.

takes strength of mind as well as application. As a competitor you need to practise concentration. This seems an odd comment, but so many archers lose concentration two thirds through a shoot. They have practised hard for the first half, they have settled and are not quite onto the home run of the final ends. Their mind wanders. They begin to chat. They are late up to the line. Sometimes, it is not as obvious and the mind merely drifts off – bored at concentrating on a small yellow dot under halogen lights. The body tires too. Only competition practice will really solve this.

Sustenance

How, when and what you eat during shooting is relevant, but very much depends on your metabolism. It also depends on the weather.

Remaining hydrated is a must. This keeps the mind active and stops the muscles getting fatigued.

Snacking during the day is good, but avoid high fat foods that give highs and lows. A big midday meal can sometimes mean you feel sluggish in the afternoon, whereas a bacon sandwich on a cold day can really set you up with energy and carbohydrates for the day. Fruits such as bananas or nut and fruit snacks are slow burners so are much better foods to snack on instead of crisps and biscuits.

If you are on a weekend tournament make sure you eat a balanced meal of carbohydrates and protein at the end of the first shoot day. Just having a pizza is not the best energy for a full next day's shoot. Neither is arriving on the field having had nothing but a fizzy drink or a coffee.

Common problems

Most problems in archery arise from instability or imbalance. As you grow more experienced as an archer you will learn to recognize problems and notice them in fellow shooters.

The draw

High or 'illegal' draw

When you first draw a bow it is natural to raise the bow high and pull the string down into you as you draw. This makes it easier to pull. It is called an illegal draw because it can actually be quite dangerous. An accidental release from a bow angled upwards can send an arrow sky high and well over safety distances. Most coaches spot this early on and correct it quickly.

Leaning back during the draw

This habit is an easy one to adopt, but a difficult one to break. The bend back invariably comes from the waist and so will vary slightly each time you draw, which will introduce a huge variable to where your arrows land on the target.

Concentrating on keeping your central core and front arm strong should solve this problem. Get a fellow archer or friend to watch you too. It is very clear to someone watching if you are not standing straight when you release. This often happens when the archer begins shooting at longer distances. If you find you are lifting your bow to aim at a far distance, try instead to draw back as normal but then angle your hips toward the target rather than using your waist or altering the angle of your arm. This is easier to replicate and does not change the angle of draw.

Putting weight onto the heels

The physical pulling of the bow can push you onto your heels. An overlong arrow can also cause this issue. You need to stand up straight during the draw and the release; otherwise your shot becomes unbalanced and your arrows will go right and left. Make sure your weight is evenly placed on both feet. Some archers roll onto their toes to settle their weight evenly before they begin the pre-draw.

Front shoulder rising

If you draw using only your pulling arm and have little or no force pushing through your front arm, you may find your shoulder starts to rise. This problem can sometimes arise if your bow is too heavy for you. If you cannot get through the clicker it is often because your front shoulder has risen up causing a foreshortening. Try to maintain focus on the push of the draw as well as the pull, which should help correct this.

Tensing up

Gripping the bow

We often learn to shoot a bow by holding it. Holding the bow can cause all sorts of torqueing that usually sends the arrow right and left.

This is a very difficult problem to rectify, especially since we are often not even aware our hands are gripping the bow. It is good to get a fellow archer to watch you as you shoot. Oftentimes it seems the bow is falling from your hand, but in truth you are pinching it between the thumb and first finger. The bow still falls away, but sometimes not as fast or is sometimes canted one way. Again, it comes down to feel. You have to train yourself to become acutely aware of what different parts of your body are doing. Try a longer finger sling for a little while to make sure you really are letting the bow fall forward.

Arched back

If you do not keep a strong core during the draw, tension can appear in the back, creating an arching inwards of the lower back. This can be easily recognized because the bottom usually sticks out. It can be common in thin, weaker archers, especially women.

Kissing the string

The body is lazy, so this problem can easily appear. Instead of drawing back, the head moves forward to kiss the string. Sometimes it can just be the lips that reach forward to kiss the string, but even they can make a good few millimetres difference. To solve this you have to concentrate on your back tension as you draw. It is usually a simple one to solve once someone points it out.

Arm and hand position

Moving your bow arm

When aiming, it can be common to move your arm to the target to aim. This creates a change of angle that will invariably be inconsistent. Instead, keep the bow arm straight and lean from your hips to correct the angle and bring the target into view. This is easier to replicate and maintains the angle of draw.

Curling your fingers

Often when concentrating on aiming you forget about the push and pull of each shot and squeeze your fingers around the string to help draw through the clicker. This is common when you begin to tire too. This problem can also come from a poorly fitting tab that does not suit your hand.

Bent wrist

The wrist should be straight. If it is bent then the elbow is usually open, or angled outwards, rather than in alignment behind the arrow. On release, the elbow will move down so the force and direction of the arrow does not follow the extending line. Sometimes this is caused by the archer trying to align the string with their nose using their fingers rather than tucking their hand into their chin.

Anchor and release

Holding an anchor

The anchor should not actually be an 'anchor' because you should not be coming to a stop, but a slowing down of action. It is common to draw your bow quickly, because the fluidity helps the action, stop once you have reached your anchor point and then aim. This nearly always results in a tiny forward creep, often just millimetres, but those millimetres will be enough to throw your arrow up and down from yellow to blue at the furthest distance.

A clicker can help with the problem, although this is not really what a clicker is for. It is best if you concentrate on your release and follow-through.

Releasing early

It is common for a beginner to release the arrow before being on the centre of the target. This just takes time and practice to correct. As you gain more control over every aspect of your form you will find you have more control at the aim.

Trying too hard is usually the reason for this. Thinking too much can result in a loss of fluidity. Attention goes to the hand rather than on the whole of the shot. This often reoccurs when archers begin competing because they are concentrating so hard on getting things right.

Letting the string go (or the Queen's wave)

Your body wants the easiest answer so just letting go when you think you are in the right position is much easier than following through.

Sometimes an archer pulls the bow with their fingers and their arm muscles rather than their back muscles. This is especially common with stronger archers. In this instance, when the hand reaches the point of release the archer just opens their fingers and lets go. When the hand moves to right behind the head it can be the body faking the release. The fingers are opening and moving out of the way of the string a split second before the whole arm moves backward. You can get very consistent form with this method, so often it can only really be detected by an experienced archer watching you closely or through slow motion filming.

Over-aiming

Over-aiming really means hesitation, and hesitation leads to incorrect expansion and poor grouping. Over-aiming can often occur at near distances purely because you feel you should be able to hit the centre with every arrow. You have to trust your practice and yourself. Try not to over-concentrate. Bare-boss shooting can sometimes help relieve this problem.

CHAPTER 7

THE NEXT STAGE

More about the bow

Limbs

Bow limbs transfer stored energy into the arrow; therefore their construction is rather critical to how the arrow flies. Good limbs can be shot for years and years, which is why there is much discussion over what limbs perform the best.

Previously, we mentioned the different construction of limbs. There are three types of limb: laminated wood, laminated wood with carbon fibre, and carbon fibre with syntactic or composite foam core. (There is also the fibre-glass limb, which is especially common at the lower end of the market.) Wood limbs have been around for years and are strong limbs that are best in constant temperatures. Foam limbs make a stronger core that is more durable, more consistent in variable weather conditions and is widely held as being a more forgiving limb. Due to the construction the foam core limbs are also considered less prone to twisting at their tips – generally the weakest point in a limb. The carbon limbs with maple wood core are also gaining in popularity.

Smooth draw

There is a lot of talk about the 'feel' of a limb. Let me help explain what archers mean by this. A bow should feel smooth to draw. A smooth draw makes your bow easier to control, which makes it easier to achieve a repeat performance, which is want every archer is aiming for. As you slow down to come to your anchor point this smoothness should remain. Sometimes, some bows start to feel slightly heavier as you reach your anchor point. This is called 'stacking'. It can arise from a mismatched bow, where the limbs are being overworked, or sometimes from just being an old or very cheap bow.

Snappy vs soft release

Then there is the release, when the string is released from your fingers and the limbs

Many archers on the shooting line.

move forward, sending the arrow on its way to the target. Archers often refer to the release as being 'snappy' or 'soft', by which they really mean quick or slow. A snappier limb usually feels a slight bit sharper on release. Certain limbs are known to be softer than others. For example, Hoyt are often described by archers as being soft, whereas Border limbs or Ukhha limbs are commonly seen as snappy.

HANDY HINT

If you are struggling to reach distance with your poundage then a snappier bow may help give you slightly better sight marks.

PERSONAL TIP

I have shot W&W, SF, Ukhha, Border and Hoyt. I prefer the softness of the Hoyt for Olympic style competition which shoots about 180 arrows on a given day, but favour my Border limbs for field shoots where I will only shoot 60 arrows a day.

When to change limbs

Once you have been shooting for a year or so, you will want to find an optimum limb weight that suits your strength. Shooting the highest draw weight you can happily control results in a faster arrow (the lower trajectory for the arrow denotes less time in the air for it to be affected by winds) and a cleaner release. As a consequence, however, you have to shoot more often to maintain your strength and therefore your control. Choose something that suits your regularity of shooting.

PERSONAL TIP

Like many archers, at the end of my first year, I went up in poundage. Immediately, I found my form was all over the place. I fell out of love with my bow. A disaster. No surprise my scores dropped substantially.

Ignoring everyone's advice , I dropped back down in poundage to my 26lb limbs and persevered, and did make Master Bowman.

Archery is so related to your own physicality and determination. Be confident in what your body is telling you, because you are the only one on that shooting line.

Risers

As we mentioned earlier you can combine different size risers with different length limbs to aid your shooting. If there is not enough bend in the limb then there will not be much stored energy to pass on to the arrow. If there is too much bend the limbs can stack. Interestingly, in the US many hunters want a small bow to carry through the woods and shoot quickly, so many risers are 15'' or 17'' risers with limbs, which make a bow of only 57in.

Grip

An archer can shoot using a low, medium or high wrist position. The medium and low position is popular because it is the most relaxed position and keeps the hand stress-free. The angle of a high wrist position can put undue pressure on the wrist, which may tire and cause you to torque the bow, especially after a lot of arrows.

Kim Yu Mi, European Archery Festival shooting with low wrist position.

Stabilizer systems

It is best that on the arrow release the bow travels forward in a straight line, but then really it is up to you to discover what you like the bow to do immediately after you have shot the arrow. Some archers like the bow to spin quickly away from their hand, whereas others like the bow to lose all momentum as soon as possible. If the bow is too front-heavy it will drop away – if it is too light it will not. The best way to check this is to get a fellow archer to stand at the side and watch the long rod as you shoot. The long rod should move forward and drop away. If it flicks upwards then try introducing some weight; if it drops away early try taking off some weights.

Rubber dampers are common and stop the force quickly. However, you will see a lot of variation of weights and their combinations in various positions on the bow. Nowadays, with more modern bow construction techniques, bows have less vibration and so need less dampening. Different trends come and go: at the moment Brady Ellison, under the tutelage of Coach Kisik Lee, is currently shooting with long side rods and no dampers; the idea is that by eliminating the oscillation caused by dampers a steadier period of holding, prior to release, is enabled.

More about arrow shafts

When you start shooting longer distances regularly, the type of arrow you shoot becomes more important. It is most probable you will want to move on from your Jazz arrows!

Arrows in boss.

Aluminium

The aluminium arrow, invented in 1939, was used in the Olympics right up until the 1990s. The aluminium arrow is actually the straightest arrow you can buy and, as we mentioned earlier, are tough little friends to have in your quiver. They are made in a wide range of spines, so are commonly seen at every club.

Alloy/carbon mix arrows

These shafts are lighter and thinner than

Stabilizer system.

Brady Ellison, stabilizer system.

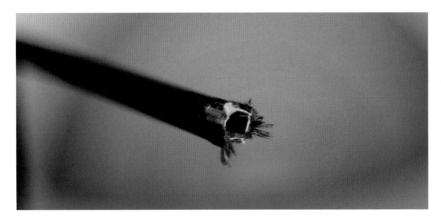

Split carbon arrow.

their aluminium counterparts, and so travel faster to the target on a much more direct route, making them less susceptible to wind. Alloy/carbon mix arrows consist of an inner aluminium core wrapped with carbon fibre, so they are actually more irregular in build than an aluminium arrow. This can easily be seen when you look at a split arrow. Although stronger than aluminium arrows, they do suffer stress and crack, usually at the point end, so get into the habit of regularly checking them.

ACCs

ACCs are a very popular carbon mix shaft. These are solid, hardwearing arrows that are quite forgiving across the range of recommended poundage, which makes them quite easy to tune. They are also fairly hardy so generally last a couple of seasons. They are sold in single units too, so you can easily top up a set rather than fork out for a new batch every year.

ACEs and X10s

Competitive archers often progress on to the more expensive ACE and X10 arrows. The shafts of these arrows are barrelled, meaning they taper from the centre to the back of the shaft (which accounts for their cost). The design makes them much more efficient in flight. The X10 is smaller in diameter, but heavier than the ACE, which makes it much more robust and aerodynamic in windy conditions. X10s only come in batches of eight or twelve so

it is more costly to sustain a good shooting set.

ACGs

There is also the ACG, which is pretty much an ACE without the barrelling. All of these carbon mix arrows are sized in spine, which is related to how much bend the actual shaft has. In addition there is also a batch coding that refers to the actual weight. By requesting a matching batch number an archer can get the closest match to the arrows they prefer and can fine tune more easily.

Pure carbon arrows

These shafts are lighter in weight and

so shoot faster, but lose velocity quicker, therefore often are not as popular for longer distance shooting. Many UK archery ranges, whose fields are used by schools or for other sports, do not allow pure carbon arrows to be shot because they cannot be located with a metal detector, and so if lost they leave a hazard to other users.

Indoor arrows

Archers often shoot their outdoor arrows indoors because the tuning process is complete and they are familiar with the feeling of their shooting. However, shooting a small target at close distance results in a much higher chance of arrow casualties! It is sometimes wise to change to a cheaper arrow.

The aluminium Easton Eclipse X7 shaft arrows are the alternative indoor choices. Larger in diameter, they stabilize in flight much quicker than their carbon counterparts, especially if fletched with large feathers, so make an excellent choice for an intermediate shooter. They are also very easy to tune. Easton's Fat Boys are a popular carbon choice since they are even lighter, as fast and much wider. Their pure size may win you a few more line cutters and therefore a few extra points, which all counts at the scoring end.

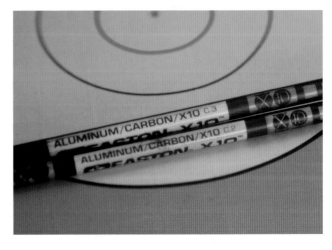

C marking batch codes on X10 arrows.

Arrow accessories

Once you are shooting relatively good groups, the actual spine of your arrow also becomes more critical and you will find yourself playing around with point weight, nocks and fletches. Each of these components can help in keeping your group tight, especially at the longest distance during variable weather conditions.

Mix of fletches, points, nocks.

Fletches

Fletches should maximize stability and minimize drag. If the arrow flies dead straight then the fletch follows, but if there is variation then the fletch starts to help steer the tail of the arrow back on course to follow the arrow tip. (Hence, if your bare shaft flies straight, then hopefully the fletches are doing the least work needed.) The larger the fletch, the quicker the arrow steadies out.

However, this also means the arrow has more drag and flies slower. At longer distances you may see the arrow 'drop off' as momentum dies down. Feathers are mainly used for indoor shooting because of the high drag of the feathers but lightness of weight, which can help weaken the spine and helps tune fat aluminiums! Outdoors, you usually want a faster arrow for optimum performance.

Plastic vanes

Plastic vanes are very popular and durable for all types of archery. They come in all sorts of lengths, heights, types, shapes, thickness and colours: Easton, Plastivanes, GasPro, Bohning and so on. High profile vanes can sometime cause clearance issues, if the arrow or the vane catches on the bow or arrow rest. Generally, this shows up as torn fletches, erratic arrow flight or poor grouping at near distances.

Spin wings

Spin wings help spin the arrow as it flies. They come in both directions, right wing or left wing, which is the way the arrow will spin. Right-handers should choose right-handed spin wings and left-handed, left spin wings. Do not combine! Each colour is a different weight and degree of stiffness, which is why when shooting spin wings archers use the same colour for all three fletches. White is the softest, then yellow, red, blue and then black. Spin wings also come in different lengths and profiles. The length should be dictated by the arrow speed. If you find you have a parachuting effect at your longer distance you need a smaller vane. Normally, the faster the arrow the smaller the vane should be.

Spin wings are attached to the arrow using strips of tape rather than glue. The best setup to begin with is to lay your arrows on a flat table, turning each nock so the widest gap of fletch is facing the table and will end up facing toward the bow.

Spin wings often need to be shot to be tuned, which involves shooting the arrow

Plastic vanes in target.

Fletches in correct position.

Spin wings and wraps on arrows.

and turning the nocks to make sure you are getting proper clearance from each arrow. If you are getting arrow clearance issues, dust a little dry foot spray or talcum powder on your bow window, arrow rest and arrow, and see if your arrow leaves marks after it has been shot. Or pop some lipstick on the edges of your vane (a little messy!). If there is contact it should show up as scuff marks or leave a mark where it hits the bow.

Eli vanes

Eli vanes are similar to spin wings in that they rely on a helicoidal shape with a curl, but they are lower in profile. These are proving to be very popular in competitive archery, maybe because each vane has a 'tail' at each end which makes them easier to apply to each arrow. These vanes also come in different colours, but with no variant of weight or stiffness so you can choose any colour combination you like. P3 is recommended for target archers.

Finding the best fletch often comes down to testing out what flies well in different weather conditions, so it can be a time consuming activity, but can also be fun. You can practise shooting good arrows whilst playing around with different types and colours of fletch.

Arrow wraps

Wraps are popular because they allow you to personalize your arrows, which helps identify your arrows on the target. You can also get wraps with line markings in place for fletch placement, which makes fletching much, much easier and quicker.

Points

Arrow points are measured in grain weight, varying from 80 to 120. It is best to begin with the recommended point weight for your arrow, which will be located on shop websites or the arrow manufacturer's site. Tungsten points are the most expensive: small but heavy, they are popular with elite archers because they literally drag the arrow through the air at speed. They are also very durable. However, they cost a lot of money.

Break-off points are prevalent with intermediate archers. Break-off points come in two weights: 80–110 or 90–120. Each point is sectioned so you can break off the weight, choosing 80, 90, 110 or 90, 110, 120. These are ideal when tuning your arrows since you can select variable weights and then shoot your arrows to see which fly the best.

To test out which arrow weight works best divide your arrows into two groups of different point weights, making sure you mark clearly which arrow is which weight. (It is easy to forget to do this and then realize you are unsure which arrow has what weight point in it.) Shoot your arrows to see which weight points group the best. With point testing it is best to test the outcome in both calm and windy conditions.

You are looking for the heaviest weight that still enables you to shoot your furthest distance with a comfortable sight mark, although Coach Kim apparently advises 120 grain points for every arrow, even if this means bringing your sight in at the furthest distance.

Spin wings, Eli vanes, vanes.

Nocks

Nocks too come in different sizes to fit different strands of string as well as different fittings for the size of arrow shaft. A uni-bush or nock pin needs to be inserted into the end of the arrow shaft to enable the nock to be fitted on to it, with the size of pin or uni-bush needing to match the arrow shaft size. Again, do your homework before purchasing. There are insert nocks, pin nocks, in and out nocks. Pin nocks and over-nocks are well liked because they stop the arrow from being split if – and when – your arrow gets rear-ended by another.

You will hear a lot of target archers discussing Beiter nocks. These nocks are produced from a single mould that results in incredibly high precision. (I have heard archers talk of their visit to the Beiter factory as though it were something out of Charlie and the Chocolate Factory!) The asymmetric nock also means that it has the best fit to the string as it is pulled back for release. The match is to the Beiter nocking point, which can be served onto your string. The Beiter website shows in clear detail how to do this.

Although a small component, nock types can alter the stiffness of the arrow due to a difference in weight or length of ear. For example fluorescent nocks weigh less than full colour, and long-eared nocks will weaken an arrow more than short-eared nocks.

Beiter nock and Beiter nock point.

Nock point

The bow grip is not actually in the centre of the bow; there is an imbalance. The position of the nock point corrects this disparity by making sure the limb tips are at the same point at release, which sends the arrow on a straight and true path to the target. Therefore, the position of your nock point is entirely relevant to how you hold the bow, with what pressure and your hold on the string. Your nock point should end up where it is best for the arrow. It is fine either high or low as long as it is within the middle section of your bow scale.

Beiter nocks

When you are shooting a lot of arrows per week, you will find floss nock points start to undo a little too often. Most archers either progress on to Beiter nocks or else serve on their nock points. I find the Beiter nocks are fiddly to put on because you have to redo your whole serving and then, if you change your brace height – for example if you are tweaking your bow or form – you have to change the nock point too which is counterproductive since you have to serve on a new nock point or walk the serving up or down, which takes ages. Served too tight, Beiter

Nocks.

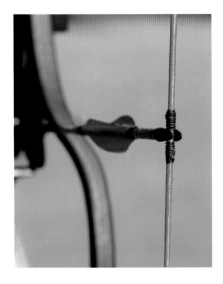

Served on nock point, Korean style.

nock points can crack; served too loose they can move. On balance I would say the Korean nock point is best for ease and lack of effort.

Other accessories

String

Strings can really affect performance. Strings with more strands create a slower string and more forgiving release. Those with fewer strands are faster but can be more erratic on release. There are many types of string.

Materials

Dacron is often sold with a first bow and was invented in the late 1950s so has been around a good while. Dacron tends to stretch with each shot which gives a forgiving release, hence good for beginners, but removes energy being sent to the arrow, so is considered a slow string by many archers.

Fast Flight is a common material of choice which is easy to get hold of and is a very long lasting string.

BCY Dynaflight, made from a material originally designed for marine ropes, is strong, durable and has less stretch than dacron.

Another more recent string that has proven to be widespread on the archery range is Giga. This string has no stretch and is very fast, but is perhaps a little less forgiving than other materials, so you may find it makes your bow a little noisier on release.

Angel Dyneema is a less common, light string that is liked by many competitive archers because it feels smooth, mostly down to the fact that it is not waxed and provides excellent consistency. However, remember that nothing in archery is constant. This is especially relevant to strings because of the variety in material.

Strands

Some strings are thinner than others and so will affect your strand choice. For example, a BVY-1825 16-strand string transposed into BCY-1827 material becomes a 20-strand string. So do some research or ask around before buying or having strings made, as some strings are specific to compound bows and may not be as suitable for recurves. There are always new options on the market and generally most strings are not too expensive to try out.

Colours

Strings also give you a creative way to personalize your bow with single colours or multi colours. Do bear in mind that colours will affect your string picture. Darker colours appear thinner, and brighter colours appear wider when up close to the eye. Sometimes a darker colour works well outside, whereas under fluorescent or sodium lights a brighter string can be more clearly seen.

Tab

There are many tab choices on the market. The type and style comes down to what you feel comfortable with. Some archers prefer square ends, others like angled bodies that fit into their palm. Some prefer finger spacers or shelf tabs. What is important is to find a tab that fits the size of your hand and allows for your hand to be relaxed throughout all stages of the draw and release.

Materials

Many shooters modify their tabs for comfort. The faces on a tab are adaptable. You can easily add more leather to your tab for more finger protection, or swap in other materials such as Oberon which is much more cushioned.

Leather is very popular, but takes a lot of arrows to shoot in. Leather can also become cold and slippery in the rain (and rain is common in UK shooting) which can cause a clumsy, even painful release. After wet shooting, leather dries very hard and so needs a number of arrows to bring back the suppleness.

Vulcolan, a rubbery material, is less common and more difficult to find to purchase, but needs no shooting in and is

---

PERSONAL TIP

I like the darker colours, because I found the brighter string became too dominant in my field of vision when I was aiming at far distance. So strings are definitely a choice of preference.

I have also found different colours have different properties. A yellow string shot slower than my black string. I get my strings made, and try for uniformity. I always order two of the same coloured strings at the same time in the hope the maker will make them together from the same batch of material.

Personalized tabs.

completely weatherproof. Although some archers say the texture feels 'sticky' and slow. Again, it is all a matter of personal preference. Try out what you can.

Pressure button

The universal thought is that the Beiter button is the best, but it is expensive. Hence, most shooters opt for other brands depending on their bow make and finances. The Shibuya DX is incredibly popular and long-lasting. It also comes in many different colours. (Grub screws can fall out, so it is advisable to have a second button in your bag.)

Button check.

Button check, push in.

You can buy button pressure gauges, but I find the simplest method to set a replacement, or back-up button, is to push them against each other. Using your eye put the band in the same place on both buttons, then put them together but pointing in different directions. The band and ends should be similar. If there is a little gap turn the band until they are even. Now put the plungers together – button to button – and press. You want both button plungers to move against each other evenly. If the new button moves inward before the other then it is weaker, so stiffen the plunger. If your original button moves before the new button then weaken the new button.

Clicker

A clicker is a point of reference to let you know when you have reached the same draw length. This is the first instance of something you actually want to make a noise on a bow! You need a clean sound. I find metal clickers are cleaner sounding than the carbon alternatives, which can be very quiet so that once on a shooting line with a number of archers with lots of clickers you might not hear it. The other factor is that once you move onto carbon arrows you will not want metal scraping on metal, so do choose a clicker that has a plastic tip. Remember, do not cut your arrows to fit your clicker; move your clicker to fit your arrow!

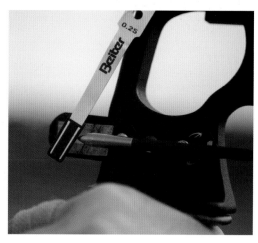

Clicker.

How to set a clicker position

Warm up a little, then get someone to watch for where the tip of the arrow is, just prior to your release. Over the course of twelve arrows or so see if there is a consistent place that you are drawing to. If there is not, then perhaps it is too early to set a clicker. If you are relatively consistent, get your friend to set the clicker to this pre-release position.

Now shoot another twelve arrows, but ignore the clicker if you can (difficult, I know). Hopefully you will find that you either click through the clicker and still draw back a few millimetres before firing the arrow, or that you shoot before the clicker has clicked. (This may tear your fletches off so it is probably best to get your friend to err on the forward position when setting things.) If you are conscious of the clicker you may find you struggle to pull through the clicker.

Move the clicker back or forward until it feels about right. It is helpful if your friend can continue to watch where your arrow tip is, to help you. It is amazing how a little move can make a huge difference. It can seem like you are pulling a bow 100lb heavier! As you get used to your bow, you will most probably find your draw length increases and you can move your clicker with the change of your form.

Do not be a slave to your equipment. If you are struggling to come through the clicker just move it forward a little. You and your body vary day to day – so use your equipment to help you rather than rule you. Warm muscles on a sunny day stretch easily, whereas when you practise on a freezing day, dressed in lots of layers, cold, tight muscles can be less mobile. Some archers refuse to change their clicker, but really, sometimes moving your clicker forward by a millimetre or two can turn what would have been a frustrating day of struggle into a productive and enjoyable day of shooting.

Fine tuning a bow

By all means tune your bow and enjoy doing so, but it will never give you the points that working on your form can give you. Improvement of technique can push up your score by 50+ points if you are committed to working on your shoot shape. A basic bow tune is really fine until you reach Master Bowman classification.

However every archer is looking to gain those easy points, so here are a number of methods of fine tuning. Some archers use them all, some archers not at all. An archer I shoot with, who regularly puts in Master Bowman scores, never fine tunes; in fact, he shoots with a button as rigid as a rock.

Arrow problems

Initially, there are a couple of things to look out for when arrow tuning.

Fishtailing

When your arrow looks like a fish when it flies through the air – the back end

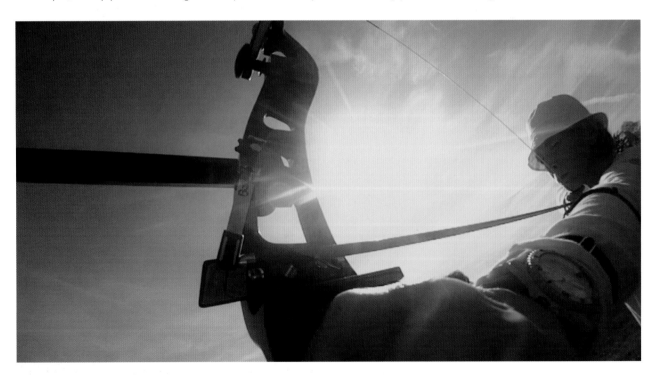

Sun shooting.

wiggling all the way to the target – we call it fishtailing. This is usually down to a mismatched spine of arrow.

Porpoising

When your arrow appears to wobble up and down as it flies through the air, this is porpoising. Commonly, this indicates a clearance problem, that is, a part of your arrow is catching on the bow as it is shot. Oftentimes, it is the fletches that are catching, but clearance problems are usually caused by shooting an arrow that is incorrectly spined for the bow weight.

The simplest bow tune

The simplest tune that is very reliable is the bare shaft tune described in Chapter 3. Choose the distance you can comfortably group at or where your arrows happily will land in the red. If this is below 20 yards then perhaps leave tuning until you are a little more competent. It is best to tune to your shooting distances. If your distance is between 70m and 30m begin your tune at lowest distance. If tuning for indoors then bareshaft at 18m, because most competitions are around that distance.

Once you have shot a nice group of fletched and bare shafts at your shortest distance, move on to a longer distance, say 50m. Shoot all your arrows. If they have plenty of room on the boss then move to 70m and shoot all your arrows. If your arrows are on the edge of the boss at 50m then it means they will probably shoot wide at 70m and you are in danger of shooting off the boss, so keep your tuning to this distance until they centralize. Once at 70m, tweak your button pressure until the bare shafts and fletched arrows group well and central.

Once happy with that, return to 30m and repeat the sequence going back and forth between the distances until you get the straightest line you can between each distance. Although this is not the most precise tune it certainly sets up your bow to a good foundation that suits your shooting.

Matchstick method

The slightly longer methodical tune is the matchstick method, which was initiated by Rick Stonebraker. For this, you need a notepad, a matchstick and some time.

- First, remove the button from your bow. Unscrew the button and remove the spring, but keep it safe! Replace the spring with a piece of matchstick that is very slightly shorter than the spring. Then put the new, stiff button back in place.
- To begin, put an arrow on the string and set your centre shot. Instead of having the string just to the right of the arrow, move the button so that the arrow is directly in line with the string. This is usually just half a turn or so. Now shoot your fletched arrows into a boss at 18m, adjusting your sight pin until you are aiming, and all the arrows are landing, in the centre of that target.
- Now replace the matchstick with the original spring in the button and adjust the button so it is back on centre shot, so the tip of your arrow shaft is to the left of the string again; a quarter turn of the button ring is normally all that is needed. Shoot again at 18m, but adjust the arrow placement by changing your button pressure. Do not adjust your sight pin. If the arrows are to the left of centre then take a little pressure off the button, whereas if the arrows fall to the right, add a quarter turn or more to stiffen the button plunger. Keep adjusting the pressure until the whole group are where they were when the matchstick was in place.
- Now shoot at 70m with your fletched group. See where your group is. Turn the pressure by half a turn either right or left. Note where the arrows go and the size of the group. It is often useful to take a picture on your phone.
- Add another half turn or full turn and do the same, making notes of how many turns you have made as you go. At some point your groups will begin

to widen up. Reset to your original position and turn the button the other way. Once again, there will be a point when the group opens up. Choose the best group and set your button to that pressure.
- Return to 18m and shoot your arrows again and look at where your bare shaft ends up – most probably somewhere different from the main group. This is fine – your arrows have tuned themselves at 70m! The furthest distance is the most critical. If you can get the best group at 70m you should be all right at 30m.

PERSONAL TIP

I have found the Rick Stonebraker tune can sometimes result in a harder button setting than I like. A softer button is more forgiving when you make a poor release, so I sometimes revert to the simpler tune. It really depends on how well you are shooting.

Keeping it in perspective

It is quite easy to get caught up in chasing bow tune perfection, which in truth, can sometimes be an elusive creature. Although it is good to know the rules, ultimately archery is not a finite sport. On any given day the form of an intermediate archer will vary, in body and mind. Even a twisted bow can still shoot consistently. Once you start shooting well you should get to know the feel of your bow and what is working well. Tuning is all about getting your bow to work with you to give you the most confidence when you are on the line. If it starts to create insecurity in your kit, then seek advice or stop tuning and just shoot. Rules are also made to be broken. Break them and see if you shoot better!

Other tuning methods

These methods are recommended by many other archers, although I find them either laborious to organize or producing an outcome not quite so reliable as the bare-boss tune.

Walk back test

Place two bosses together. Mark an aim point on the top boss and walk back about 5m. Set your sight and shoot your first arrow. Without moving your sight pin, continue walking back, shooting an arrow at every 20m, always aiming at the aim point.

The arrows should fall in a straight line. If, as the distance increases they fall right, then increase the stiffness of your button. If they fall left then decrease the pressure and soften your button a little. Sometimes, shooting a few arrows at each distance will give more accurate results; otherwise as you shoot from further away your form can affect the arrow placement.

Paper tuning

To my mind this is not really worth the effort, but do not let that put you off!

Put up a frame with a large piece of paper attached to it one metre in front of the boss. Stand about 6m back from the target and shoot your bare shafts through the paper and into the target.

Inspection of the tears should give you an idea of the arrow flight: a tear up from the main arrow hole means your nock point is too high, so the arrow has gone in low and the nock has entered high; a tear down means your nock is too low.

Once this is corrected shoot again. A left tear means the bare shaft went in on angle to the right, which means the arrow shaft is weak; if it is a right tear it means the arrow is too stiff.

CHAPTER 8

FURTHERING YOUR FORM

To improve as an archer you need to be honest with yourself about what you would like to achieve, what time you have and what commitment you are willing to put in.

Your practice

The best way to improve is to practise, practise, practise. Actual shooting is the only way to get feedback on your shooting and help you learn with each shot. The more you shoot the more you become attuned to the small changes in your body.

You do have to be open to understanding yourself as a sports person. Every archer has a strong and weak part to their form; a strong bow arm but weak release, or vice versa. The best archers work hard on smoothing out their flaws. If you spend time and concentration on improvement your body will learn to feed back to you with more detail. This in turn will help you locate and correct problems more easily. Set your own goals that are realistic and achievable.

It is fine to want to shoot in the Olympics, but make an achievable step plan to get there, beginning with what you want to achieve this season, this week, this shoot session. Sensible goals help

Olympics 2012, Lords, London.

maintain enthusiasm, optimism and a sense of achievement which is good for your mental approach and therefore your shooting.

Building confidence

Believe in your bow, but most importantly believe in yourself. It is surprising how confidence can help you reach your goals quickly. Shooting three or more times a week for a few hours is a good start and will show improvements quickly. Top archers shoot over two hundred arrows a day and follow a rigorous fitness regime. They also have team mates, coaches and constant feedback.

Even so, ultimately archery is a sport of the individual. So plan your practice to what suits your character. As you gain strength and arrow fitness you can build up your arrow count. A good purchase is an arrow counter. You will be surprised by how few arrows you shoot sometimes, especially if you are exercising your chatting muscles on the line instead of shooting. It is also no good banging out huge numbers of arrows if you are not concentrating on making each arrow a good one – you will only reinforce bad habits.

Lonely shooter.

Quality practice

Like most sports, archery is all about the quality of practice. Some days you will shoot badly. Accept the bad arrows, but remember the good ones. Practise more when you are shooting well – it helps reinforce the muscle memory.

> **PERSONAL TIP**
>
> Even shooting every day I find I need about one week of solid shooting for a few hours each day to change something in my form. Select one thing per session to improve.

I often see beginner, and intermediate, archers keeping score every single time they shoot. This is a bad habit to get into because it puts your focus on the end result and not on your shoot style. Do concentrate on your six-end average and try to better that.

Arrow counter.

> **PERSONAL TIP**
>
> If you are scoring a round and are not doing very well, a cheeky little cheat that is good for morale is to shoot another end and add up, for example using that last score rather than the poor middle one. (Obviously you cannot do this if you are putting in the result for classifications!) It sounds silly, but it helps take the concentration off the numeric and allows you to keep up momentum and maintain optimism.

Warm up exercises

The shoulder is a complex joint of muscle, bone and tendons with a great range of motion, so you must respect its complexity. It is very common to pull a tendon, and they take a good while to recover, so something to be avoided.

Warm up stretch.

10. As above, but put your draw arm a little higher than usual so that your draw hand is above your head. Now draw the band back to behind the head and hold for five seconds before releasing.

Warm up band.

Warming up before shooting is a must. A stretchy band is very helpful. Do all the exercise for six repetitions and make sure your shoulders do not rise up but remain relaxed throughout.

1. Tip your head to one side and hold for a count of ten. Repeat on the other side.
2. With your hands down by your side make small shoulder rotations, ten forward then ten back.
3. Reach over your head by curving your arms and bending sideways, keeping your hips facing forward.
4. Using the full length of your arms swing each arm in a big circle, forward and back.
5. Stretch out both arms to the side, forming a T with the body, and with palms facing outwards and fingers upwards draw small circles with your hands. Repeat in both clockwise and anti-clockwise directions.
6. Keeping your arms up and outstretched, twist from the waist sideways to the left, at the same time bending your right arm at the elbow in toward your chest and turning

your head to the right. Come back to the centre and repeat, turning to the right.
7. Find a sturdy vertical, like a doorway. Bring up the right arm to elbow height and put this against the doorway. Take a step forward with the left leg and lean your body forward until you feel the stretch in your shoulder muscles. Turn around and do the same with the other arm.
8. Take the stretchy band in both hands wide apart and lift your arms above your head. Now stretch the band outwards so your arms are outstretched in a T shape. Hold for five seconds before returning to above your head and repeating.
9. Using the stretchy band like a bow, take one end in your bow hand and one in your drawing hand. Draw back the band to your anchor position, but keep the head looking forward, and hold the anchor point for five seconds before releasing. It is good to do this with a weak band and then to double the band so it becomes more difficult.

Ways to practise

Build in variety

Archery can soon become boring, especially if you are working on a difficult to correct problem. Many clubs always shoot set distances with set target faces, but you do not have to follow this. Vary face sizes and target faces. Put smaller targets at longer distances. Use playing cards, balloons or pictures. Whatever brings enjoyment to your shooting. Work on your form one day, just shoot another day, then tune on another.

Distance
Some archers shoot 70m all day long, believing that the shorter distances will be easy if they have nailed 70. In truth, each

distance has a different mental approach, so shoot the distances you need to shoot in competition, but make sure you practise the distances you are not good at as well as those you are.

Sight
Use this practice time to get to know your sight. It is good to know how much the adjustment on your sight or your windage affects your arrows. In a competition you can lose valuable points from not knowing how many turns will bring your arrows back to the gold.

Timing
If you are training for competing then replicate the restrictions in practice so you are prepared. Time your ends to make sure you are shooting six arrows within the required time.

Using a scope
Use a scope to aid your shooting. Do not use it to check on every arrow. Try to feel each arrow and guess where they went before looking in the scope. If you shoot arrows and guess where they went and what they felt like, hopefully you will eventually recognize the 'feel' of a good arrow.

Aiming off

Learning to aim off during is great practice for your shooting and your mental approach. This will become very helpful in windy conditions. Aiming off is much more difficult than you think, because subconsciously your mind wants to place circle on circle. Oftentimes, you will find your eye is drawn to the gold just as you release, or sometimes toward a bunch of arrows in the target or a tear in the target face.

Choose specific points on the target that are off centre and aim at those. You can start by placing a target pin somewhere on the target so you still have something else to aim at.

As you become more proficient you will find you can be more specific with your aim. Start by aiming in the blue or black, but as you improve challenge yourself with precision. Choose the edge of 8 or 9.

You will probably find that the closer you get to the centre gold, the more difficult aiming off becomes just because your body tries to centre everything on

Arrows in the gold practice.

Practice shooter.

the moment of release. It is actually quite encouraging to find just how skilled your body is at putting circle on circle. Knowing your body is trying, despite your efforts, to place those arrows in the gold can quite often give you confidence and trust in your release.

Aiming at different points within the 10 ring on a Portsmouth face indoors is good practice for this skill too.

Bare boss shooting

Bare boss practice involves shooting at a blank boss at a close distance without actively aiming. Blank boss can be great when you are trying to work on an isolated piece of your form, such as not grabbing the bow. Bare boss shooting can be done from about 5m to 15m. Do not shoot at too close distance, because a wrong or bad hit can cause an arrow to jump back from a boss.

Once you free your brain from aiming and stop worrying about where the arrow will land, then you can concentrate on your form. This practice is all about 'feeling' the shot. The body and mind are very good at recognizing when something is out of place, so it is good to learn the feeling of executing a great shot. Try closing your eyes when you shoot. Feel each part of your shot cycle.

Close shooting is also good for building strength and learning control. As you shoot try and extend the holding time before you release. Work on the arrow coming through the clicker at the desired time. Make sure you are feeling the muscle groups in your back working, rather than your elbow or arm. Vary the number of arrows and length of holding, building up from three seconds to fifteen. Release only after the appropriate number of seconds, but be careful not to allow this to turn into a habit of holding on anchor.

Bare boss is valuable in learning the art of good arrow release, but too much shooting without a target face can make you lose focus on the act of aiming, which is crucial in successful shooting. Therefore combine bare boss with regular practice.

Bareboss shooting.

Oftentimes, it is good to shoot bare boss at the beginning or end of a day's shoot.

Home practice

If you cannot get to a range there are a number of ways you can exercise at home. Some archers shoot short distances in their garage at home or their hallway. Be careful, however. An archer I know bought a target, set it up on the back of her bedroom door and shot her first arrow. It completely missed the foam target, hit the door and bounced right back at her, missing her head by millimetres.

Understanding the weather

Rain and heavy air pressure push the arrow down and so will lower your sight mark. A very close, very hot day can

Home shooting in garden.

will blow the arrow right or left and sometimes lift it also.

Dealing with gusty wind is the most problematic. It helps if you can shoot quickly. This is really when your other senses can help you out. Normally you can hear the gusts approaching, and can get a sense of their length and strength. Listen to the trees. Feel the wind approach. Try to time it so you are not drawing just as a huge gust is about to envelop you.

Trust yourself to make good decisions. Your mind is surprisingly apt at judging wind. If not, you will find you try to hold the anchor for too long and shoot poor shots anyway. The ability to aim off can really help when shooting in windy conditions, especially if the winds are variable. Otherwise you get into a dance of constantly changing your windage until you don't know where you are when the wind drops. It is easier to adapt your point of aim rather than keep moving your windage all day.

When in a competition in windy conditions some advise looking at where other people's arrows are going in the target, that is, all left or right. I find this very unhelpful. You have no idea what poundage other archers are shooting, whether they are aiming off or have changed their windage. Just

sometimes also cause the arrows to drop, whereas a fine, dry day can lift them. If you want to be a serious competitor then you cannot be a fair weather shooter. You need to practise in the wind and the rain. Shooting in the wind helps you shoot in the wind! Obvious I know. Here are a few helpful hints when figuring out the wind.

Wind

Follow the direction of the arrow. If the arrow drops, lower your sight. If it moves right, then move your windage in to correct it. Oncoming wind will make the arrow drop, whereas wind from behind or the side can lift the arrow. Side winds

If you want to be a serious competitor, then you cannot be a fair weather shooter.

concentrate on what you know, which draws on all those arrows of practice. Relax too. Of course, the wind will sometimes blow a good arrow off course, but it can also blow a bad arrow back on course.

Record keeping

Shoot diary

Keeping a shoot diary can help you work out what areas you need to work on. It can also give you reliable feedback on the results. This diary can be set up to suit you. Some archers document everything from the number of arrows they have shot to what they ate and how they slept. It depends how serious and methodical you are as a person. The main things to note down are your arrow count, the weather, what you are working on to improve and what you learnt at the end of the session. End every input with a positive.

Filming

Setting up a camera on a tripod and filming yourself shooting can be a great way to analyse your form. You can shoot from all sorts of angles. There are quite a few apps, such as Dartfish or Coach's Eye, that can help you study your execution.

Slow motion photography can really help reveal habits you never knew you had. Nowadays most coaches are on the line filming their students, even in competition, sometimes even looking back at the footage between ends.

Practise, practise, practise.

Aida Roman being filmed by her coach during competition.

CHAPTER 9

COMPETING

'I'm not good enough to compete.' This is ostensibly untrue. Archery competitions vary from club shoots to world competitions, so there is always a shoot to suit. Most competitions are good fun with friendly competitors. Competitions help challenge you and focus your mind on your shooting, which can really help you improve. It can be rewarding to see how your practice can come together on a day when your score matters to you.

However, do not go into competitions expecting huge leaps in your score. The pressure and concentration may gain you some points, but generally you will put in your best scores on your home turf, when you are relaxed and among friends.

Competition shoots

Archery shoots vary from club friendlies right through to the National Ranking series or the UK selection shoot for Olympic archers, and take place all over the UK. Archery outdoor season runs from April until September with the most popular rounds being the 1440 WA round (which used to be the FITA Round), the 720 Round (used to be the FITA 70), or the imperial rounds: the York, Hereford and Bristol I-V. Other shoots, such as the American, Windsor or Nationals among others, also take place throughout the season.

From October through to April, competitions move indoors. In the UK you will find the Portsmouth round shot at 20 yards is the most common,

Large outdoor shoot.

whereas across Europe the WA 18 and 25 are the only indoor rounds shot in competition. The less common, and often less liked, Worcester round – which is a white spot on a black target face shot at 20 yards – can sometimes pop up as an odd inter-club friendly contest.

Types of shoot

There are three categories for competitions in archery, which all, according to Archery GB, should be shot with 'Union, Trueheart and Courtesie'; these are: non-record, record and world record status. Non-record status are rather relaxed shoots with local judges, whereas record status shoots are a little more stringent, and have a regional judge presiding over the events. World record status shoots are run to the highest standard of judging that adheres to very specific rules.

At record status shoots, countdown clocks or traffic lights are used to time each end, and all archers must have their equipment checked over by a judge on the morning of the competition to make sure everything is in order. Every arrow must be numbered, marked with your name or initials and have the same coloured wraps, fletches and nocks.

World record status means that in any competition across the globe every archer is shooting with identical restrictions, so if a world record is broken – and I have been at shoots where that has happened – then the score is immediately recognized. There are not many sports where you can find yourself competing on the same target as an Olympic medallist.

All tournaments are split into senior and junior or cadet events, which are classed by age and sex. Some tournaments have distance awards, age awards and team awards as well as the usual gold, silver and bronze positions. A junior can, and often does, enter senior distances, and men often decide to shoot the 'women's' distance during some of the

Koreans Kim Yu Mi and Park Se Hui are placed first and second at European UK stage, after going to a second one-arrow off.

A scoreboard of almost perfect scores.

Aida Roman, Olympic silver medallist, with target mates.

further distance rounds such as the York and Hereford. Competition shoots are really for what you feel up to rather than what you should shoot.

All archery competitions are run under World Archery (metric) or Archery GB (imperial distances) rules. The difference between the two often causes confusion, even for a seasoned archer, so let me explain how the rulings differ.

WA – metric distances (once FITA)

In WA competitions there are normally four archers per boss, divided into shooting pairs labelled A&B and C&D. Each pair is called a detail. The first detail shoot first, followed by the second detail, but you alternate which detail shoot first. Archers go up to the line on a whistle or horn sound and have ten seconds to settle themselves before shooting. Another horn or beep will announce shooting can commence. Each detail

shoot six arrows in one end at the further distances and then, at the shorter distances, it drops to three arrows per end. (This is just to stop too many arrow casualties.)

There are some 1440 WA shoots, where the closest distance is shot using an 80cm, 5-ring face which enables six arrows per end to be shot because two targets per boss can be used. The lowest scoring arrow is a 5. This makes the afternoon run faster, but also means that a few points may be lost if you make a silly mistake or have a bad arrow, because a shot that may have been a 2 effectively becomes a miss because the black and blue rings have been removed.

In a WA round, you should mark the target face with two tiny marks where every arrow has landed before pulling the arrows out of the target, but most shoots are happy with one line. (Remember to mark the misses. If you get a bouncer you do not want it to look like it is the unmarked miss !)

In WA you are given a set time within

which to shoot your arrows. For six arrows you get four minutes and for three arrows two and a half minutes. You will shoot to a countdown clock or traffic lights. With thirty seconds left to shoot the traffic lights will turn amber until the horn or two beeps signal time is up. If you shoot your arrow after this time you lose your highest scoring arrow, as you also do if you shoot before the commencing horn has sounded or if you shoot more than your allotted arrows.

Once the allotted time is up the horn sounds twice and all archers move off the line. Normally, once you have shot you will move off the shooting line unless you are the second-to-last archer. If that is so, you wait until the final archer has shot all their arrows – just out of politeness. When you are the last archer shooting, it is actually a great comfort to have another archer waiting with you on the line. The more competitive archers, who are chasing scores for their target rankings, or practising for international competitions, favour the WA competitions. This is because the imperial rounds are actually much more difficult to achieve great scores on, due to the most arrows being shot at the longest distance. A windy day can make a huge difference, whereas in WA round competitions you can often make up the score on the nearer distances. This also means that, as a general rule, Archery GB shoots are often a little more relaxed overall.

Archery GB – imperial distances (once GNAS)

Archery GB shoots often do not use countdown clocks, although the same timing rule applies. They also allow six archers to one boss or three archers to a single detail. Like WA rounds, you shoot in two details and alternate who shoots first, but the first archers only shoot three arrows before stepping off the line, making way for the next detail to shoot their three arrows. The first detail then return to the line to shoot the next three arrows. (I have never been at a shoot where this has not confused someone!)

After you have all shot six arrows you score and collect, with no need for target markings.

Practice or sighters

WA and Archery GB rounds also have different rules for practice or sighters in competition. Outdoors, under World Archery rules there is 45 minutes of practice, which generally works out at about three ends. You can shoot as many arrows as you wish within this time. For Archery GB you get six sighter arrows only. In indoor competitions, under WA rules, you can shoot as many arrows as you like in the allotted practice time, and if you are shooting a double round you can practise before each actual round. Under Archery GB rules you only get two ends of three arrow sighters, and if you shoot two indoor rounds you only get sighters on the first round – even if you change target numbers. Confusing eh? Wait until you begin shooting them!

Competition day

On arrival at the competition field you will need to sign in and check your position on the target list. Most competitions produce an online target list a few days beforehand, but last-minute changes do occur so it is best to check. Most competitions start with an assembly, where the judges are introduced and the rules of shooting are stated. The start time will be on the entry form. Sighters are usually after assembly but not always, so do check. The entry form will also list if catering is available.

Food and clothing

A lot of archery shoots do not provide much in the way of food, so sometimes it is best if you bring your own food and hot drinks. There is often a small barbeque simmering in adjacent competitors' tents, so be prepared to have lunchtime announced by the smell of sausage and bacon floating across the waiting line. You should not wear blue denim, camouflage clothing or strapless tops, and no open-toed footwear. One competition my fellow competitor, a young cadet, was not allowed to shoot because he was wearing camouflage shorts; luckily, he was able to swap trousers with his grandfather who had driven him there.

Many archers set up tents behind the waiting line and set their scopes on the line. The four archers on each target usually agree amongst themselves where the best placement is for the scopes and whose scope has the best optics. It is common practice to share scopes, with the best scope winning pole position. If you do not have a scope it is always polite to ask the owner if you may use theirs – they never say no.

Competition day chaos.

Setting up at a competition.

Scoring at a competition

Score sheets can appear daunting at your first competitive shoot, even if it is a friendly. Sometimes, some archers take advantage of a newbie and avoid picking up the score sheet so the new archer is forced to keep score. The actual rules state that the C shooter should be the scorer, but most times people take turns or agree among themselves who scores and who pulls arrows. Do not be afraid to say you would prefer not to score or to suggest everyone takes a turn per set distance. No one should write down their own score, so you will pass the score sheet between you anyway. Indoors, you will often have to cross score, with each detail scoring for the other.

In a competition, the most important thing about scoring is to write down the correct arrow score that has been called out. You can make all sorts of mistakes in the addition, but once the arrows are pulled from the target you cannot change the arrow score value. It is good practice to repeat the numbers out loud as you write them down, so you have three witnesses listening. If you do make an error call over a judge

Score sheet corrected by judge.

and they will correct it. All mistakes on the arrow value have to be corrected by a judge. There are always mistakes so do not worry about calling over a judge. I have written down the wrong number, put the wrong number in the wrong place and even put the arrow score onto someone else's score sheet! It happens.

Only archers who have shot can go up to the target, or in the case of archers who have disability or illness, their agent will go up. Do not touch the boss or target face until all arrows have been scored. A line cutter gets the highest value. Call the value you believe your arrow has scored. The other three archers should agree; if they do not, feel free to call a judge to get them to take a closer look. It is quite amusing to watch them scrutinize your arrow under a huge magnifying glass! It is always good to synchronize scores with every archer at every distance end. That way if there are any errors of calculation it can be sorted out over the tea or lunch break. At the end of the tournament check your own score sheet because this is what you are signing as a final. Nobody minds you tallying up so do not feel self-conscious about double checking.

Competition rhythm

A competition is not the time to practice your form. It is the day when all your practice should come together.

Nerves

Competitions often induce nervousness. These normally come from wanting to do well. This is a natural instinct so accept it. If you have done all your practice and feel prepared there is nothing more you can do except enjoy the challenge. In

GB archer Amy Oliver under a sun umbrella.

a competition routine will anchor you in calmness. You will see many archers on the shooting line go through their shoot tick. This is especially obvious when archers are under pressure. If a shot goes badly you will see the archer collect themselves in a number of different ways. Some take a moment to rest their bow on their foot and gather their concentration, others realign their shoulders or reset their grip, replace their arrows or make a fine adjustment to their finger sling whilst others reset their hair or hat. Use whatever you need to help bring about calm and concentration.

Social or solo?

Try not to compare yourself with other archers. Try not to look at other targets. You can guarantee that when you do, you will see a bunch of arrows in the gold or see an archer release a perfect loose. You can also guarantee that you were not looking at them when they shot their miss. It may be the only X they have shot all day.

Many competitors talk about their form or their faults, or often offer advice on your shooting. This can distract your mind or start you thinking about your faults. In a competition you need to be positive, optimistic and resilient. If this means you need to sit on your own in your tent, then do so.

Archery is not a team sport. At the end of the day, it is up to you to ensure you do what is best for you to both enjoy the competition and do well in terms of your own expectations. Depending on your personality you will find that there is a balance that suits your shooting; some archers are chatty and sociable whereas others seek solitude and concentration inside their own tent. Hopefully, you will learn after a few competitions what you prefer.

PERSONAL TIP

I like the act of putting on my finger sling just before I am about to step up to the line to shoot. It signposts the beginning of my focus.

I also always keep my finger sling, arrow puller and tab in my quiver and when I shoot put my tab in my trouser pocket, so I know very quickly if it is missing. You will not believe how often a dropped tab is found on the field. Some archers like to leave their tab hooked on the end of their long rod, but if it rains then it can become soaked or you find you put it in a different place that is unfamiliar.

PERSONAL TIP

Shoot each distance as well as you can. Once the distance is over, forget it – and the score with it. I got into a terrible habit of thinking the competition was won or lost by the longest distance, so if I shot a poor long distance would almost have given up for the second half of the day. It took a good month or more of actively working to halt this mode of thought, but as soon as I did, I shot much better at the shorter distances.

Settling in

The fact that rounds are timed often freaks out new competitors and can cause heart palpitations. In actual fact, four minutes is quite a long time in which to shoot six arrows. If it is windy, try to shoot your first arrow in the first thirty seconds. This helps alleviate a tension that can build from thinking about the little time you have and the amount of arrows you have.

Use your sighters to help settle your form. Some archers prefer to shoot a lot of arrows to warm up, others prefer to shoot for precision. Shoot a good few arrows before you alter anything. It is best to get a group and feel you are shooting well, rather than change everything after every sighter. Remember you can move the group – if you do group! When you are outdoors, use your sighters to learn about the weather. These are the arrows you can afford to make mistakes on, and mistakes can often tell you something. For example, if the wind is gusty choose the gustiest time to shoot and see where your arrow ends up, or choose this time to aim off during the gust. When you are being timed and are forced to shoot in the gust you should have a better idea of how far your arrow will be blown off course, or of where you need to aim to stay near the yellow.

In competitions there is often a leader board. This is sometimes placed at a central point within the shooting area and so is unavoidable to see. Try not to build up strange superstitions around scoring such as not looking at your score. As an active competitor you should be honest with yourself and know what you are capable of achieving. On the practice field you will have been shooting an end average, so should know how this compares with how you are shooting on the day of competition.

Be flexible

Also, do not get fixated on always wanting to shoot on the right or the left. You will start looking at the target list ahead of tournaments and start telling yourself you will not shoot well because you are on the wrong detail. Practise on the field to unsettle yourself until you are happy shooting on either detail.

Learn to shoot through distractions. Sometimes in a tournament you find yourself shooting very close to others who may have all sorts of habits that can divert your attention if you let it. I have shot with incredibly vocal shooters who curse themselves and everything else through every shot; archers who intake breathe so heavily you would think they would suck you backwards; archers who comment on your arrows, your score and your form; and archers who seem to set up some sort of personal competition against you for the course of the shoot. You can always blame these disruptions, but at the end of the day it is only you, the target and the wind on the line.

It is up to you to tune out interruptions and become single-minded on your aim. If you do shoot a bad arrow do not even bother looking in your scope. Gather your thoughts and forget that arrow. It has gone. There is nothing you can do about it. It is easy to tell someone not to dwell on bad arrows, since we tend to say to ourselves 'if only...we hadn't shot that 6 or missed that end or noticed the arrow wasn't on the arrow rest properly'. You will never lose these thoughts, but you can train yourself not to dwell on them. Becoming a competitive archer is about lessening the time it takes you to come back from that bad arrow.

Moving your scope

In Archery GB shoots, which are more likely to have a mix of target, barebow and longbow archers shooting, you may find someone on your target asks for you to remove the scope for when they shoot.

Scopes are allowed on the shooting line, but only in agreement with all shooters. This is their entitlement. Firstly, try and place the scope out of their way, but if they are insistent then mark where your scope goes and place it on the line before you shoot. Leave your scope at the edge of the line, lined up so it is quick to move in place. You will worry at first about losing time, but you have ten seconds to settle on the line and normally this is enough. You should not really have to rely on your scope anyway, so you should feel confident that after your sighters, you can shoot as well as you would do with a scope.

Dealing with the unexpected

If something is going to go wrong you can guarantee it will happen at a competition! So be prepared and do not be surprised.

Equipment failure

My arrow rest has broken, my nock point has slipped down my string in the rain, my tab has come apart, my sight pin ball has dropped out into the grass and my long rod has flown out of my quick release mid-shot. When something happens, do not panic. Just put your hand up, step a foot or two off the shooting line and call over a judge. Do not interrupt other shooters. Explain the problem and the judge will normally allow you to try to fix the problem whilst the other archers finish shooting.

Once the problem has been fixed you will be given a set time to shoot your other arrows. This often means you are required to shoot your arrows after everyone else has shot. The judge will stand behind you and will tell you how long you have to shoot your remaining arrows – normally forty seconds per arrow. This has happened to most people I know, so remain composed on the line and do not worry about people looking at you. It often feels as though the whole field is watching, but most times they are busy chatting about their own shooting or thinking about their own form rather than yours. Once you have shot the field will resume normal practice.

Extra arrow

If you accidentally shoot an extra arrow by mistake then the highest scoring arrow is deducted from your score. To shoot or not to shoot? This is a dilemma. However bear in mind that if you have only shot five arrows, then you have dropped 10 points. If you shoot again, you will more than likely shoot an average arrow. Whereas if you have shot seven arrows rather than six, even if you lose a 10, you will probably only lose a few points instead of 10 had you not shot an extra arrow. Make sense? I hope so.

Bouncer

A bouncer is an arrow that bounces off the target. If this happens in an Archery GB competition, shoot the rest of your arrows and call over the judge. They will mark an arrow's fletch and then get you to shoot that single arrow after everyone else has finished shooting. The judge will then accompany you to the target to make sure the original arrow did in fact bounce out of the target. If so, you will then get the score of the marked arrow you just shot. Sometimes a bouncer has happened by shooting into the back of another arrow – this is shown by a broken nock; if this is the case you will get the score of the broken up arrow.

In WA tournaments, if you shoot a bouncer, stop shooting and call over the judge. The judge will halt shooting at the end of that end and accompany you to your target to check for an unmarked hole. (This is why you should mark every arrow hole.) You will then return to the shooting line and shoot the rest of your arrows.

Becoming a regular competitor

County shoots

Your club's county will organize county shoots and select archers based on their

Shooting in competition.

previous scores. If you wish to be selected for the county then make sure you submit competition scores to your club's records officer or send them to the county contact, which is usually found on the county website. Your records office will keep the county contact informed of good scores. Let people know you would like to be selected. Keenness and availability on the shoot day can often mean you will get to shoot.

Target ranking

Archery GB publish a national ranking each year. To gain UK ranking you need to submit two WA 1440 and three WA 70m round scores from either world or UK record status shoots that have been shot during a single summer season. You also have to take part in an Olympic round or head-to-head shoot. You do not have to submit the score from the head-to-head, but you do have to put yourself into that

competitive setting. The form can be found on the Archery GB website. It can be exciting to see where you are placed alongside other UK archers.

Olympic rounds or head-to-head shoots

A head-to-head is the standard Olympic round. A 70m qualification round takes place first, from which archers are ranked and placed into an elimination head-to-head pairing. Archery is not normally a high adrenaline sport, but head-to-heads really have brought excitement onto the field. In archery competitions the challenge is between you and the target. In a head-to-head you are shooting against an opponent in a clear-cut knock-out round. Now, it is not just about the best archer winning, it also comes down to a little bit of luck too – the wind can gust just when you shoot, or your opponent can have a duff shot that loses that end.

The actual head-to-head round is a knock-out stage where archers compete against each other on a one-on-one basis in three sets of six arrows. Each end results in a win, draw or lose. The winner is the first archer to reach six points. A win gains 2 points, a draw 1 each and a loss 0. If, after six ends the score is a draw you go into a single arrow shoot-off. Each archer shoots one arrow, with the highest scoring winning. This takes place until there are four archers left forming the final and semi-finals of the day.

Head-to-heads require a different mental approach. Lots of

County shirt.

competitors suffer nerves. There are a few top archers who do not do well at head-to-heads because nerves and insecurity kick in. In the warm-up area you will sometimes see these archers bare-bossing to concentrate on their form and stop target panic.

I find head-to-heads great fun. When shooting with experienced team shooters they will often ask what side you want to shoot on, because they are happy shooting on either side of the line. You will also find they do not comment on your score or get in a strop if they lose an end.

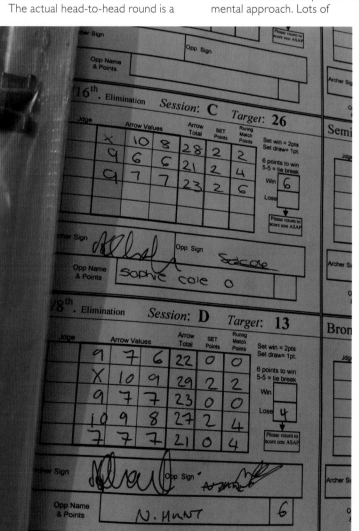

Head to head score sheet.

Target gold.

Keep your manners. It will keep you calm. And to your opponent you will seem sure. Aggression doesn't really help you in this sport, although there a few archers such as Alan Wills who needs high adrenaline – however, his aggression is not outward. There are some archers who like to unsettle their opponent.

Shoot the best you can, but certainly be competitive in your mind. You have to want to win; otherwise you will give up your shots. Concentrate on what you need to do. How you handle a head-to-head comes down to your personality and mental strength. Most archers prefer to shoot first. It takes strength of mind and practice to not look at where

your opponent's arrows have landed and not have that affect your shot. (I have seen good archers collapse in one arrow shoot-offs when they see that their opponent's arrows have landed in the gold.)

I go with the rule that the best archer will win on the day. So good luck, and enjoy!

French archer Thomas Faucheron celebrates an indoor win.

Targets in the mist.

Olympic celebration – Ki Bo Bae wins gold.

GLOSSARY

Archery is full of jargon. Here are some of the commonly used phrases and informal terms you will hear on the field.

all gold end   An end where all arrows are in the gold.

anchor point   The point at which the bow is fully drawn and the draw hand reaches the position for aiming.

assembly   A meeting prior to the shoot where the judges will go through practicalities and introduce themselves and the day's shoot rules.

at full draw   The point just before the arrow is released.

barebow   A recurve bow without sight, sight marks, clicker, mechanical aids or stabilizers.

bare shaft   An arrow free of fletches.

best gold   A prize given in competition term for the nearest centre arrow.

boss   A shooting target, often made of straw or foam.

bouncer   An arrow that has hit target and bounced out.

centre serving   See **serve/serving**.

custard   Slang term often used by long bowers for the gold on a target.

detail   The grouped archers going up to line in competition.

draw weight   The poundage of the bow.

dry fire   Term for firing your bow without an arrow in it.

dynamic spine   The stiffness of an arrow as it moves through the air; necessary to agree with your bow set-up.

end   The round of arrows shot; the standard is six arrows per end.

fast   Term shouted out to halt shooting.

fletch   The steering aid fixed to the back of an arrow, usually three per arrow.

field captain   The person in charge of shooting on the line or in a competition.

flock of seagulls   Term for an end when all your arrows have missed the target and flown elsewhere.

force line   The direction of force behind the arrow.

form   An archer's shooting style.

gold   The yellow coloured centre of most target faces.

good line   Term used when the arrows were right on course for the centre, only a little low or high.

head-to-head   An Olympic round that consists of knock-out rounds between pairs of archers.

ILF   International Limb Fitting.

in the bow   Term for when the arrow is just about to be released and the archer is central to the push and pull.

limbs   The upper and lower 'arms' that fit into the bow to fire the arrow.

line cutter   A scoring arrow that cuts the line between two scores.

miss   A miss or, in scoring, a non-scoring arrow.

nock   The back end of the arrow, which clips onto the string.

nocking point   The point on the string where the arrow is best placed.

on your fingers   A slang term describing the actual weight you are drawing, taking into account your bow weight and arrow length.

para lever   A style of limb fitting.

pile/point   Front tip of arrow.

poundage   The weight an archer is drawing.

pull   To remove the arrows from the boss.

release   The physical sending of the arrow from the bow.

riser   The handle of the bow which the limbs attach to.

Robin Hood   An arrow shot directly into the back of another.

round   A recognized number of arrows at a set distance or distances.

sag   Downward curve caused by pressure.

serve/serving An extra piece of thread or string wound around the bowstring to stop it from fraying. Often called centre serving.

sight An addition to the bow that assists in aiming.

sighters Practice arrows that help you work out the sight mark of a distance.

string Bow string.

spider The X or very centre of the target face.

static spine The stiffness of an arrow (see dynamic spine).

take-down bow A bow composed of riser and limbs, rather than a one-piece solid bow.

target face The paper face fitted onto a boss.

tiller The relative bending of bow bow limbs.

draw a bow To pull the bow string back ready for firing an arrow.

nock an arrow To clip an arrow onto the bow string.

worst white A prize given in competition for the arrow furthest away from the gold.

FURTHER INFORMATION

Useful Archery Contacts

Archery GB
Lilleshall National Sports Centre,
Newport, Shropshire TF10 9AT
T: 01952 677888
www.archerygb.org

World Archery
Maison du Sport International, Avenue de
Rhodanie 54 1007 Lausanne, Switzerland
T: (+41) 21 614 3050
www.worldarchery.org

Archery Europe
www.archeryeurope.org

Field Shoot Organizations

GNAS Field Archery
www.gnasfield.co.uk

English Field Archery Association
www.efaafieldarcher.com

National Field Archery Association
www.nfas.net

INDEX

OTHER RELATED TITLES FROM CROWOOD

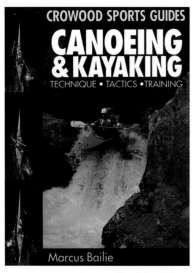

CROWOOD SPORTS GUIDES
CANOEING & KAYAKING
TECHNIQUE • TACTICS • TRAINING

Marcus Bailie

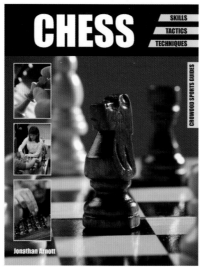

CHESS
SKILLS
TACTICS
TECHNIQUES

CROWOOD SPORTS GUIDES

Jonathan Arnott

GOLF
SKILLS
TRAINING
TECHNIQUES

CROWOOD SPORTS GUIDES

Matt Stables

CROWOOD SPORTS GUIDES
MARATHON
AND HALF-MARATHON RUNNING
SKILLS • TECHNIQUES • TRAINING

Steve Trew

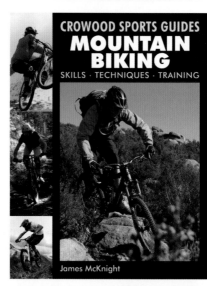

CROWOOD SPORTS GUIDES
MOUNTAIN BIKING
SKILLS • TECHNIQUES • TRAINING

James McKnight

CROWOOD SPORTS GUIDES
ORIENTEERING
SKILLS • TECHNIQUES • TRAINING

Carol McNeill

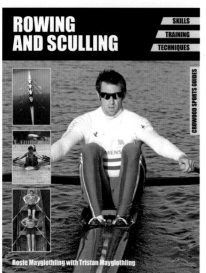

ROWING AND SCULLING
SKILLS
TRAINING
TECHNIQUES

CROWOOD SPORTS GUIDES

Rosie Mayglothling with Tristan Mayglothling

SNOOKER AND BILLIARDS
SKILLS
TACTICS
TECHNIQUES

CROWOOD SPORTS GUIDES

Clive Everton

2ND EDITION

TENNIS
SKILLS
TACTICS
TECHNIQUES

CROWOOD SPORTS GUIDES

Jeremy Woods